Congresbury Station Waiting Room
sketch by Michael Greaves

The Ghost Train and other true railway tales from the Strawberry Line

Edited by Faith Moulin

© Faith Moulin 2015

Published December 2015 by Chez Moulin Publishing

ISBN 978-0-9563747-2-1

Printed by Taylor Thorne Print Ltd

CONTRIBUTORS

Reg Bray
Arthur Cockram
Derek Craven
Colin Forse
Bernard Hatherell
Mike Lyall
Ron Oddy
Alan Staddon
George Stockham's wife Doris

I am very grateful for the support I have had from rail enthusiasts locally, particularly Trevor Riddle who read the draft and gave his advice on technical matters. I am also very grateful to Lois Brenchley for historical information about the Strawberry Line, Sandford Heritage Trust and Winscombe Old Station; Yatton Local History Society; Michael Greaves for allowing me to reproduce his sketch of Congresbury Station Waiting Room, and Mike Horwood, who kindly lent me the photos of the trains stuck in the snow at Draycott in the winter of 1963 and others of Lodge Hill station.

My family has also been a great help in the production of this book: my husband Tony has helped with the photo captions and technical information; my son-in-law, Andy Pester, designed the brilliant cover image and my son, Christopher Moulin, an academic memory researcher, gave his professional view on reminiscence.

Above all, I would like to thank all the wonderful railwaymen who have generously encouraged me and shared their experiences with me.

CONTENTS

The Source of the Stories

My friend Sue Grant and I first met with local retired railwaymen in 2000 when we were organising The *Strawberry Special*, a Millennium Festival event. It took place on the Strawberry Line (the disused Cheddar Valley line) in June 2000 with activities and displays at the former station sites in Congresbury and Yatton, North Somerset, and at various points in between. The event aimed to celebrate the history, natural history and cultural life of the former railway and one of the key components was a recording booth at each station in which people with memories of the Cheddar Valley Railway were invited to meet, chat and have their reminiscences recorded for posterity.

I was busy with other projects and when Sue died in 2002 I put away the tapes. By that time they also included recordings of other railway workers whom Sue and I had visited in their homes. I also recorded Colin Forse giving a local talk in Yatton in November 2000. We had wanted to record their memories 'before it was too late' and although it was a task we did not finish, at least we made a start. It was another eleven years before I finally got round to listening to those tapes.

In 2006 Colin Forse asked me if I would help him write down his memories. He was a great story-teller but he found the organising of his thoughts on paper difficult. We were both very pleased with the result of a year of collaboration, *A Life on the Railway*, (now out of print.)

I found Colin's stories fascinating. His career on the railway had matched almost entirely with the period of the nationalised railway industry. He was a union representative with ASLEF, one of the most powerful unions of the time. When he visited me, always off the cuff, he would tie the unhappy dog outside and come in and talk. Long disjointed stories poured out of him, some of which I couldn't understand because the joke lay in the railway culture and slang. I would write them down and then put a list of questions through his letter-box like: *'What did you mean when you talked about a banker?' 'What was the four-foot?'* It was basic stuff. I began to learn and love the tales from a life that had completely disappeared.

'A Life on the Railway' sold 400 copies and is still selling on Kindle, appreciated by railway enthusiasts and local historians alike. It raised £800 for the Strawberry Line Café, a not-for-profit organisation which has restored the old derelict Brunel-designed waiting room on Yatton station.

Colin talked about a second book, but in 2013 it was too late for him. He was too ill to marshall his thoughts and died before we could get going. But at a memorial day for Colin at the Avon Valley Railway at Bitton, South Gloucestershire, I met some of Colin's friends and colleagues, in particular the ones who had worked with him on preserved steam locomotives in their later years: Tom Jones, Graham Nash, Graham Bellamy and Bob Kent.

So began a new chapter, so to speak, of Colin's unwritten new book. I am very grateful to the railwaymen for their kindness and especially for the invitation to the retired railwaymen's monthly re-unions at the Knights Templar near Bristol Temple Meads station. A second volume based on their memories is already taking shape in my head. It has been fascinating to sit and listen to these men, whose world of work has completely gone. Their lives have been shaped by their work, by their allegiance to the Great Western Railway, (and later to British Railways) and to their workmates. Often their fathers, brothers, grandfathers, uncles and cousins were railwaymen too. They came from railway families, born and bred to serve the public through their love of steam and steel. Railwaymen seemed to have enjoyed a certain esteem among other working men. In their old childhood times every boy wanted to be a train driver: there was such glamour and glory in it, and many of these men achieved it, living and driving their dream, a King or Castle class engine on the national network.

No-one outside the industry can fully understand the life and culture in which their whole lives have been spent. No wonder they like to talk to each other! They have a common bond, a camaraderie that is unique. Where lives were at risk – their own and those of passengers – they learnt to work as a team. A driver who ignored a speed limit might be reported by a signalman or their fireman. A lazy porter at the station might delay the train, and even subsequent trains, so the guard kept notes in his journal. Their work was being checked and in their turn they were keeping an eye on the work of others because mistakes could prove fatal. Teamwork and discipline became a way of life for railwaymen.

One of the things they liked about working on the railway was its variety. In spite of the regularity of the timetables, every day was different. The job was satisfying to many because of the independence it gave them to use their own initiative and solve their own day-to-day problems. Many of these men had not been particularly well-paid, especially for the long and unsocial hours they worked, but they still felt they had enjoyed a good working life. In fact they often compared their work with jobs on the railway nowadays, commenting on the lack of job security, the lack of requirement for skill and initiative, and particularly the modern loss of a sense of duty. They got satisfaction from complying with the Rule Book, but knew, almost by instinct, when rules could be applied with common sense rather than dogmatism.

This seems not to have made the men arrogant, or boastful about their careers, but on the contrary, they are almost without exception modest and gentlemanly. In the early days most of the learning was done on the job by watching those with more experience and skill. I have enjoyed hearing them recall incidents of kindness, character and competence (and sometimes incompetence).

They reminisce, like all older people, and they know they are at the end of the line, the last of the line. There are no more railway families, nor even many life-long careers on the railway. They bitterly complain about the new management which arrived with privatisation: a management whose experience was more likely to have been gained in Marks and Spencer than on the railway. The railwaymen I talked to thought they had it better than railwaymen nowadays. In view of the evidence I have seen, they are definitely right!

I am not a sociologist so I cannot present my research using scientific methodology, but I am a storyteller, and these men have told me stories that cry out to be shared and not forgotten. They will entertain and amuse you, inform and educate you, but best of all they will leave you with a rich admiration and affection for the men who used to work on the Strawberry Line.

Many more scholarly and technical books have been written about the Cheddar Valley Line, but the descriptions in this small volume are entirely the memories of railwaymen who worked there and I have mostly reproduced them in their own words. They were not counting the rivets on the engines; they were firing and driving the engines, doing their jobs on the stations and living their railway lives. And as you will read in my son's *Foreword*, memory isn't necessarily fixed. What the railwaymen told me may not be the exact accurate reality, but we need not worry about that too much. Sit back and enjoy the tales.

Faith Moulin
October 2015

FOREWORD
by Dr Christopher Moulin

One thing that sets us apart from animals is our 'declarative' memory – the ability to verbalise, and therefore share and transmit our own personal view of the past. When this type of reminiscing is discussed in scientific circles it is often called mental time travel. Each time we recount an anecdote, or carefully preserve an autobiographical memoir or reminiscence from our past, we mentally travel back to a different time. Perhaps for the current generation, no time could seem more different than the golden era of our railways, so why do we want to go back to it? Why do we want to dwell on moments that are gone? The old-fashioned answer is that life is lived forwards, but understood backwards – memory helps us learn for the future. But memory has a social function too, helping draw people together based on common reminiscences. This book draws on what comes naturally to most people: to reminisce, to share personal histories and to weave a narrative from our shared pasts.

You don't need a cognitive neuropsychologist to tell you all this. People have spontaneously shared their memories and authors have carefully documented them from long before the advent of experimental psychology. In fact, memory scientists use the language of books. We talk of life 'scripts' to describe the common structure of our life stories, which are divided into 'chapters'. Memory researchers, like writers, know all about the malleability of stories, the polished anecdotes which shift over time, and improve with each retelling. In a court of law, or in an exam, what matters is that a memory is a reproduction of the truth. The rest of the time, however, what is important is correspondence (with the past) and coherence (with the rest of our life story). That is, it doesn't matter so much that we remember the past how it was, but that we can reproduce how it felt to be there, and what it meant. Some memories, like anecdotes, can be amalgams, exaggerations, or distortions of the truth. That doesn't concern the memory researcher, nor the writer. What's important is the narrative, the sense of the past. For me, growing up in probably the last generation that romantically wanted to be train drivers, a very important memory from my life is sitting in a cab of an HST at Paddington, and being allowed to start the engine by the kindly driver, before taking my seat in the carriage for the trip back to Yatton.

The evocative slices of railway life in this book could be the basis of scientific study, or just a good read, but in either case they enable us to go back via mental time travel to an era which is gone but not forgotten. Memories are the building blocks of all history, and these stories are a collection which brings alive a period of critical importance for British life. Memories keep alive abandoned branch lines, ways of life, and outmoded technology; memories are the new ghost trains on abandoned rails.

Chris Moulin

45xx class passes Lodge Hill Goods Shed on its way to Cheddar;
next stop Draycott.

57xx class coming into Lodge Hill.

CHAPTER ONE

The Cheddar Valley Railway (aka the Strawberry Line)

The Cheddar Valley branch line became known as the Strawberry Line because in the summer strawberry season it carried fruit from Somerset to the mainline at Yatton to be sent via Bristol all over the country. This trade had begun in Victorian times and was still big business for the railway in the middle of the last century.

Some of the railwaymen interviewed in 2000 were based on the Cheddar Valley line but many of those who worked there were based in Bristol. Ron Oddy was one of many drivers who worked all around the region. He used to enjoy working on the Cheddar Valley line. The route meant coming from Bristol to Yatton along the mainline then all along the Cheddar Valley to Witham and Frome, then back to Bristol through Pensford and Brislington. He enjoyed those circular runs but remembered roasting in the cab when it was hot and there wasn't much he could do to keep cool. If the weather was bad and the train had to go tender first (because there was no turntable to turn the engine at the end of the line) it was not a lot of fun for the driver and fireman in the cab with no protection from the elements.

In the 1940s and 1950s strawberries were picked up from all the Mendip stations right through from Mells to Draycott and taken to Yatton. The little engines would be pulling twelve wagons sometimes. The railwaymen said the strawberries in those days were tasty. Many of them remarked that the seasonal Cheddar strawberries were much tastier than the big supermarket ones available all year round fifty years later.

The strawberry season required additional staff because the Cheddar strawberries were sent as far away as Newcastle, although Birmingham was one of the main clients mentioned. 'Lads' – boys who started work on the railway from the age of 15 until they got full pay at 20, would be withdrawn from their usual work during the strawberry season and sent on the 2.50 afternoon train from Yatton to Cheddar. The yard at Cheddar would be chock-a-block with people, trucks and trolleys.

Race to the Hills

The strawberry season was the highlight of the year for local railway workers. When the strawberry vans started to arrive at Yatton and all the sidings were full up, it meant a lot of overtime pay. There were extra trains and we ran up to Draycott to load up then back to Cheddar and Axbridge and then to Yatton where the vans were coupled to the up trains to Bristol.

On one occasion the order came to take empty vans from Yatton back to Axbridge, Cheddar and Draycott for the strawberry traffic coming back. There were a lot of wagons there to be taken and it would mean two trips. George Stockham, the driver, wasn't keen on all the overtime and he asked me, his fireman[1], what I thought about taking them all in one go. I thought about it then replied, *'Yeah, why not?'*

I knew it would burn a bit more coal and boil a bit more water so I was ready to shovel like mad. It's a shame there was no-one making a film in those days. The long train would have been quite a sight charging up the 1 in 100 incline to Sandford, then on the long climb up to Shute Shelve tunnel with both injectors right on the maximum mark. We took it easy coming home once we had got rid of all the vans, but when we steamed back into Yatton with a light engine there wasn't a lot of coal left in the bunker and the shed man wasn't happy because the only way to fill coal was by hand from a wagon. I stayed to help seeing as the shed man was my father and he would be doing the shovelling!

Colin Forse

---

[1] In railway terms, the fireman's job was to make the steam to power the engine.

The 'Cheddar' strawberries didn't come just from Cheddar – they came from any of the places on the south Mendips where there were warm slopes to produce an early crop. There was a Strawberry Special – a train just for the fruit – leaving Draycott every afternoon at about 5.25 pm to go to the Midlands. The fruit wagons had wooden slatted sides to ventilate the fruit and keep it cool. They were called Siphon Gs[2] and there were other wagons known as Fruit Cs and Fruit D[3]s. All the wagons would be stencilled YATTON and transferred there just for the period of the Strawberry Specials, then they were moved somewhere else. Some of them went to Weymouth for the Channel Islands' early fruit trade. Many of them were standing idle a good part of the year.

The men doing the loading at Axbridge, Cheddar, Draycott and Lodge Hill had piles of large wooden trays to put in the wagons. They put one layer of fruit at the bottom, then the next tray had a sort of leg to it to give the lower layer plenty of room and air, and then another tray in the same way on top of that one, stacking them about four high. They couldn't pile up any more or they would have started falling about. The strawberries were loaded into vans during the day and re-loaded onto a new train in Bristol. Then the fruit wagons would be hauled back around 8 o'clock in the evening. Railwaymen would travel down with the empties to Congresbury as a lot of the fruit wagons were stabled at Congresbury in one of two sidings there. In the 1930s and 1940s there would be another Strawberry Special at 11 o'clock at night to get the strawberries to the markets for the morning, but this late train had been stopped by the end of the 1950s.

The strawberry season lasted about six weeks. Men and boys from Bristol and other stations around the area would catch a train sitting as a passenger up to Draycott to help with the loading. Then when the work was done they had to get back home from there.

[2] The Siphon G was a louvred wagon also used for milk, a 50 feet bogie van with corridor ends.
[3] The Fruit C and Fruit D wagons were 22 feet long, ventilated specifically for the transport of fruit.

No Free Taster

One day in the 1950s a Bristol fireman had offered to help load the strawberries. He didn't offer because he wanted to be helpful; he was doing it because he wanted to get back to Bristol quicker, *'all in a mad hurry'* as the guard said. This fireman wasn't putting his back into it; he was standing there waiting and sometimes moving a tray while everyone else was doing the loading work. He picked up a punnet of strawberries and said, *'Thanks mate'*. The owner of the strawberries was helping load them. He looked up and said, *'Half a crown please.'* He wasn't going to make a gift of his strawberries to that lazy Bristol fireman. The fireman was already eating them so he had to put his hand in his pocket!

Colin Forse

Loading up the strawberries. Photo by kind permission of the Strawberry Line Association.

Flowers, Grass and Greenwood Boxes

As well as the staff brought in to help, there were permanent staff based at Cheddar to load other goods as well as the strawberries. From January onwards the trains carried anemones, then Cheddar pinks and various other flowers, then the strawberries, then early potatoes. In fact they were busy from January right through to September with all the different types of goods. Doris Stockham also mentioned mushrooms.

Special trains ran from Avonmouth to Wookey Paper Mill (St Cuthbert's Paper Works) at certain times of year with grass to make bank notes. This special grass came from Mexico and was called Esparto grass. The boat would come in at Bristol City docks and, once they had started unloading it, a special train went down every day until all the cargo had been loaded onto the railway. The trains then went down to Wookey on the Cheddar Valley Line and into the paper mill's own siding. The railwaymen would stop at Wookey all day for about twelve hours, shunting the wagons about while they were unloaded. It was hard work, all day long, for three or four days.

There was general goods traffic on the Cheddar Valley Line as well, and this included wooden boxes made at Goslings Sawmill in Congresbury especially for South Wales Tinplate Works. The boxes were 2 inches deep and 2 feet 6 inches square, all in green wood, and along with them were boards to place inside the skeleton boxes which protected the South Wales tinplate in transit. A trainload of beer came every evening from Shepton Mallet – the barrels would be piled up for loading at Shepton Mallet and Wells ceiling high. Local cider was also carried by rail, and stone from the Mendip quarries was a constant.

Congresbury station had little passenger traffic but it was busy with the goods traffic. The large goods shed contained a two-ton crane used for loading and unloading and the two porters would also find it handy to lift heavy sheeting onto trucks and save them doing it by hand. The sheets and ropes were stored under the floor and accessed through a trapdoor. Before the war it was never necessary to lock the shed as goods could be left there overnight without fear of theft.

One of the most important cargoes was hay from the area around Congresbury which was sent to South Wales for pit ponies. Pit props for the South Wales coal field were also handled at Congresbury and these would be loaded by hand. A Wrington company making upholstery and saddles, Organ Brothers, was another big customer in the 1930s, both for the distribution of their products and receiving by rail sacks of rags which were made into the stuffing.

The amount of traffic increased during the war because Government Food Stores were set up in the area and Congresbury became a centre for distribution as it had the largest goods shed. A goods porter had to be employed to cope with the extra work and women were employed on the platforms as porters, and to help with the paperwork.

In the 1940s milk was carried in churns. Every farmer had his name on a brass plate on the top of his churns to be sure his empty churns came back to him. That meant a job for porters, sorting out all the names and making sure that if Reg Ware had left six churns, Reg Ware got his own six churns back. A travelling porter, based on the train, would assist in the loading and unloading of churns at every station.

Collected from memories shared at the Strawberry Special, June 2000, by Arthur Cockram, Colin Forse, Bernard Hatherell, Ron Oddy and Alan Staddon.

CHAPTER TWO

Happy Families

When boys left school and entered the railway as lads at 15 years old, they knew they might have a job for life. Many of them came from railway families and the railway was 'in their blood'. Their future lives and their own families would also be moulded by the demands of a railway job. They often married daughters of railwaymen and it was not unusual for families to have been involved in the railway for a century and a half. Railway families often lived together in groups or terraces of railway cottages and the children would know the life of early rising and shift work from an early age.

Ron Oddy had stopped working on the railway in 1955 when diesels were brought in. He had worked his way up from the signal box booking boy at Parson Street[4] Station, was a call boy[5] in 1937, then an engine cleaner. After about a year he became a fireman on a shunting engine, then progressed to firing on goods services, then local passenger services, then the mainline expresses. Finally he made it as a driver but had no heart to learn to drive diesels after a life with steam. His father had been a passenger guard and his father-in-law was a driver.

I asked Arthur Cockram if, at 15 years old, he had wanted to join the railway and he replied: *'I had no option. My father was a stationmaster and my grandfather a signalman. We had railway blood.'* Arthur's brother, Paul, was also on the railway.

Alan Staddon's first adult job (he had joined the railway in 1935 when he was 15) was at Wrington just after his 20th birthday. He

---

[4] West of Bedminster on the Bristol – Exeter mainline.
[5] People did not have alarm clocks in those days so a call boy was employed to knock on the drivers' doors at night and the early morning to make sure they got to work on time.

had finished being a lad and had to move to a vacancy as directed, or be sacked, so he didn't have much choice.

As a railwayman's son, a lot of Arthur Cockram's childhood was spent hanging around stations and goods yards. His father had been posted to Weymouth and there were pigeon trains down there with a dozen vans[6] with pigeons in. These racing pigeons had been sent the previous day from far-flung places miles away. They often spent the night in the sidings and then the birds were released to fly back to the place they had come from. Railway children used to go off in those vans getting eggs because the birds used to lay their eggs while they were in the train. It was a bonus in those lean times in the twenties and thirties to have a lovely breakfast of pigeons' eggs.

Doris Stockham joined a large railway family when she married her husband George. George's brother Reg used to drive a railway lorry in Clevedon; another brother, Bill, was a porter; Monty, a nephew, was in the signalling department; Arthur, a cousin, was a porter; Ron, a nephew, was a passenger guard; George's brother Jim was a ganger[7] on the Yatton – Clevedon line; Jake Wilmott, an uncle, was a ticket collector at Yatton.

George Stockham's mother worked in the bookstall on Yatton station and when he left school at 14 George wanted to do something on the railway. He was too young to start as a GWR 'lad' so he worked on the bookstall, disappointed that his mother wouldn't let him take charge. He was able to start working on the railway at 16. He worked cleaning coaches at Yatton to start with, working with George Parker. Then he went to the engine shed, preparing the engines. After the war he was sent to Aberbeeg in South Wales. He had to lodge in Aberbeeg in Railway Terrace – it was all railway people there.

---

[6] Special pigeon vans were like coaches but windowless and fitted out with racks for the pigeon baskets.
[7] Gangers would walk the line checking for issues. They could shelter or have a break in small, brick-built line-side huts with stoves in. They had a look-out man with a flag and whistle.

George was a fireman at that time, then when he was passed as a driver he was able to come back to Yatton when there was a vacancy. He did 58 years service. Doris was very proud of him and often said it was lovely to be the wife of a loco driver.

Recruitment was often quite informal in those days. Reg Bray's father's parents were farmers in Wiltshire but his grandfather died when his father was still at school and the farm had to be sold. Reg's grandmother got work at Westbury station as a charwoman cleaning the offices every morning. One was the office of the Divisional Superintendent of the line: R G Pole, whose brother Felix (later Sir Felix Pole) was General Manager of the GWR. When Reg's father was about to leave school, Reg's grandmother asked Mr Pole if there was any chance of getting her son a job. He duly became a porter at Freshford and that started off the railway family. When his youngest brother left school, he obtained a job on the railway in Bristol. When Reg's brother left school he started in the Operations Department in Bristol, then Reg left school and also started work on the railway. Reg's sister married a railwayman and so did his wife's sister.

Colin Forse's brother Roger worked with him at Yatton station, and in the 1950s they were there with their father Ernest Forse (Ern). Colin had wanted to go into the merchant navy but his father had persuaded him that it was a better life on the railway as he had done both.

Reg Bray said that his brother, as a lad porter, would spend at least an hour every day cleaning his brass buttons and his boots. In the 1930s he said none of the staff would go to work without a tie or a hat and you would very seldom see an untidy person on the railway. Nine out of ten guards would have a flower in their lapel. The only ones unable to keep themselves clean were those on the permanent way[8], or engine cleaners, because they couldn't do their job without getting dirty.

---

[8] The rails, sleepers and ballast were often known as 'the permanent way' because it replaced temporary tracks during the construction period. The name stuck with railway men.

The permanent way staff, the locomotive staff and the signalling department staff were all issued with overalls and an overcoat. Only the operating staff got uniforms. Reg Bray said that in the thirties he had had to buy his overalls himself and had to take care to keep them clean. He took good care not to let them get too dirty.

Doris Stockham recalled the work of washing her husband's dungarees in the 1940s using a rubbing board in the kitchen sink. They were very dirty after he had been under the engine oiling it up, but George always went to work in clean dungarees.

Happy Campers

The camping coach was an old-fashioned railway coach that had been gutted inside and painted up to provide a basic standard of accommodation. On the Strawberry Line there were camping coaches at Congresbury, Winscombe and Cheddar, with another on the Wrington Vale Light Railway at Blagdon. It fell to the porter to clean the camping coach so Arthur Cockram remembered the one at Congresbury well. It had a small kitchen cum dining room at one end and bunks for beds. Both lighting and cooking were by oil. The porter's job was to provide fresh oil and water each day. People wanting to rent it had to travel to it by train[9] and buy a certain number of return tickets to Congresbury as well as paying the rental of about £4 per week, but as it had eight berths it only worked out at ten shillings each. Some people brought a little car as well so they could get around. That gave people a cheap holiday. The camping coach was only available in July and August because people didn't get a lot of time off from work then as they do now, but it was occupied all the summer.

The railway provided all the linen and the porters had to change all the linen on a Saturday and send the dirty linen off to Swindon to the laundry. It travelled in a wicker hamper with a reversible brass label.

The camping coach didn't have a toilet and the holidaymakers would be given the keys to the station so they could get into the

[9] Blagdon was an exception as holidaymakers only got tickets to Bristol.

station toilets because the ladies' toilet in particular was in the station building. The stationmaster used to run around like a busy bee to make sure the customers and holiday-makers were happy.

Doris Stockham used to take her holidays in a camping coach. She used to go on holiday by train to a camping coach at Dawlish Warren as a member of the local Staff Association. It was regarded as one of the benefits of the job. There was a small cost, but not much. She also remembered going to another camping coach at Marazion. She said there were no conveniences, and only one stove so it was just like camping but with the advantage of a leak-proof roof. She said, *'We liked it and when you got home you could have a nice bath.'*

Congresbury Station with the clerestory roof of the camping coach visible on the right. 7th April 1959. Photo: J Harrold. (Transport Treasury)

CHAPTER THREE

The Work Force

A Line Man

In 1938 Reg Bray came to Yatton as assistant lineman[10] after working in Bristol as a lineman's lad in the Signalling Department. Mr Ralph was the stationmaster at Yatton then and he was succeeded by Mr Morgan. There were at that time three ticket collectors; two booking clerks; six porters; two foremen; a carriage cleaner; seven drivers and seven firemen in the locomotive department; two shed men, who used to clean the engines and coal them, and a gang of ten men. Not all these staff were working at Yatton every day, but they were based at Yatton and paid every Thursday at Yatton.

In 1947 Reg was working 7.30 am to 7.30 pm, cycling or walking to the signal box at Claverham from his home in Yatton. He had to know all the different kinds of telephone and circuits. There were 267 different types. His hours used to include Saturday mornings up until 11.30 am, and on 1st February 1947 it started snowing just as he got to work. He had to stay on after his normal 11.30 finish time because it was still snowing. By one o'clock the snow was so heavy that no points or lockbars could be moved in the signal boxes. He remembers having to work 18 hours a day for six weeks just to keep the points working – and that was all they could do, just keep them working. Very often during that bad winter he would leave the signal box at 10 pm, just get in bed and then someone would come calling for him again. Keeping the trains

---

[10] The line man (or linesman) was in charge of the mechanical signal apparatus and the electrical apparatus and did all the installation, maintenance and fault-finding. The assistant was his deputy.

running was paramount. Reg recalled that there weren't a lot of delays to passengers in those days. Everybody pulled their weight to keep the railway running. The permanent way staff would walk the line through the snow to put salt on the snow on the points. Passenger services took priority and if a goods train was in the way it would be put in sidings in Claverham or Hewish waiting for a passenger train. Reg recalled that if they were there any length of time the fireman would put a bucket on the signal pull so that when the signal was changed the bucket would fall off and rattle so he would wake up!

A Gentleman at Congresbury

There was a signalman who worked at Congresbury who was 'a bit of a gentleman' with gentleman's manners. He had apparently worked for some Lord and Lady at Nailsea. He used to come down on the Welsh goods train from Nailsea to Yatton and then cycle from Yatton to Congresbury to open the signal box. By the time the first Cheddar Valley train of the day got to Congresbury he would be ready to call out, *Breakfast is ready*', and he was such a nice man, so polite, that the driver and fireman just had to stop and be sociable and have breakfast with him.

This man was obviously charming to everyone, including the opposite sex, and one of his driver colleagues dropped a clanger with him once when he was travelling to Cheddar on a Sunday afternoon. The driver spotted him sitting in a carriage accompanied by an attractive young woman and said, *'Is that your daughter leaning out of the window?'* To the driver's surprise, the signalman said, *'No, that's my wife!'*

Colin Forse

A Porter

Edgar Skinner was what was known as a travelling porter. He spent a proportion of his time on Yatton station then he would travel on the train to sort the goods loaded at Congresbury, Sandford and Axbridge. He would go from Yatton to Cheddar and then get the train up to Bristol. He was later a guard along with Walt Blagdon, Ted Clark, Jim Bull and Bert Maslen. In 1938 at Yatton when Reg Bray was working there, Ralph Witton was a goods porter.

Rough Cider

Edgar liked a drop of cider and kept a quart bottle of it hidden behind the booking room door. When there were no trains coming in he would pop in there and have a swig. A guard from Taunton, Frank Ratcliffe, found out where the cider was, so he used to get off the train, have a quick swig of Edgar's cider and top up the bottle again with water. One night Edgar caught him but he didn't chastise him at all. The next Saturday night, instead of a bottle of cider being there, he put a bottle of paraffin oil. Paraffin oil on the railway was dyed a pinky colour and it looked like rough cider. The train came in, Frank sneaked into the booking office and took a swig from the bottle. That was the last time he took Edgar's cider!

Reg Bray

The lad porter learnt the job by having all the tedious or unpleasant jobs given to him. At Congresbury station in the 1930s this included dealing with the numerous oil lamps, trimming their wicks, filling them with oil, testing and lighting. The paraffin would have to be re-ordered when running low, and would be sent from stores in Swindon.

He also had the job of getting the water for the toilets. Arthur Cockram explained: 'The water had to be pumped up by hand into the tanks in the roof every day. That was a terrible job – until we had a lorry come there and there was a hosepipe supplied and a water tap installed. It was the only fresh water on the station. We devised a way where we could attach the hosepipe to the outside tap, get the steps and go up through the roof in the gents toilet and fill up the tanks with a hose instead of doing all the pumping.'

Once the men were trained they knew their jobs without the need for daily scrutiny and they became resourceful to deal with any minor emergencies that might crop up during the working day. If they got stuck they might refer to an older, more experienced member of staff, or the stationmaster if they needed approval for a particular course of action. If the stationmaster couldn't decide what should be done, he would know someone who could. Staff could also cover each other's work and this was mainly how juniors received their training. Even the stationmaster's paperwork could be covered for a few days by one of the clerks.

The resourcefulness and independence of engine drivers in particular was also heavily influenced by the strong desire to offer exemplary service to the public. It could be argued that sometimes one of the railway workers might take it too far. He could never work alone, however, and the following story is a demonstration of teamwork and collaboration, even outside of the Rule Book.

The Ghost Train

In the late 1950s the Sequence Dance Club from Yatton used to visit the nearby town of Clevedon for an evening out. One particular Saturday night, the bus on which they were to return home had broken down and one of their younger members was despatched to run to the station where the steam train[11] was waiting. The young man explained the dancers' predicament and asked the driver if he could hold the last train until the group could get there. The driver said he could not. The last train ran at 11.15 and he had to get the passengers back to Yatton. He did however, after a brief discussion with his fireman, have a plan.

'You wait there,' he said to the dancer. 'We'll come back for you.'

The last train, as scheduled, got back to Yatton, the passengers went home to their beds and the fireman was sent to the signal box to tell the signalman what was afoot. The engine was taken back to the shed and filled with coal. By this time it was well after midnight. They steamed back to Clevedon, picked up the dancers and chuffed on back to Yatton.

[11] Collett 0-4-2 tank engine fitted with an auto trailer for push-pull working.

A couple of days later the Inspector came down from Bristol and summoned the various drivers to the stationmaster's office.

'*What was going on at the weekend?*' he asked. '*I've received complaints that a train was running from Clevedon to Yatton in the middle of the night. Does anyone know anything about that?*'

'No,' the men replied. '*They must have been hearing things. No trains run after midnight.*'

The Inspector had his suspicions, and periodically over the years he continued to ask about it. He knew who was on duty that night but the men concerned always denied all knowledge of the incident.

'*It must have been a ghost train!*' they said.

When the Clevedon branch had long been closed and the driver and fireman were older and, possibly, a little wiser, the Inspector thought he would ask one last time.

'*Now tell me the truth. I'm about to retire. There's nothing to be lost now but I just need to know. You did run a train that night to Clevedon, didn't you?*'

The men had to own up. They were the crew of the legendary Ghost Train.

Colin Forse

Collett 0-4-2T 1454 pushes the Clevedon train into the bay platform at Yatton station, 28th April 1957. Photo: R C Riley (Transport Treasury)

A Carriage Cleaner

Charlie Parker was the carriage cleaner at Yatton before and after the war. His job was to look after the two coaches going in and out of Clevedon and the coaches for the Cheddar Valley line. He had in the engine shed a wooden box that was exceptionally long so it could hold the very longest of long brushes that were used to clean the carriages. They were always kept locked up, safe from theft.

In the 1950s the shed man was Jimmy Green.

A Signalman

The main duty of a signalman was to make sure that trains moved about safely. Each train movement was logged by hand in a book by the 'booking boy'. Signalmen were less directly supervised than most of the men and they could get away with homely comforts in the signal box, like taking their carpet slippers to work, or getting themselves a more comfortable chair.

One signalman (whose father had also been a signalman) said there were two signalmen who used to work in the signal box at Cranmore who had disagreed over something and wouldn't speak

Yatton West signal box 31ˢᵗ May 1969. Photo by permission of Railway Correspondence and Travel Society (RCTS)

to each other. When their duties coincided or followed one another they would leave each other little slips of paper with notes on!

Signalmen at Yatton in the 1950s were Malcolm Wathen, Charlie Francis and Len Hazell.

Mind the Hot Tap!

Some time before the war, Len Hazell, one of the Yatton signalmen, had got hold of a chromium plated tap. These shiny taps were a rarity at that time and many people had never seen one. Len used to put the one he had acquired on a gas ring in the signal box and let it get really hot. When he could see someone coming to the signal box he would carefully remove the tap from the heat and put it in a prominent position. People would come in and say, '*I've never seen one of those before,*' and pick it up. Len liked a laugh!

He didn't laugh so much when he made a table at work. He went over to Counsell's timber yard and bought some wood and made a beautiful table there in the signal box. The trouble was that when he had completed it he couldn't get it out of the door. The men had a good laugh at his expense then! You might say the table was turned.

Reg Bray

The Shed Men

The loco shed had a single line which would accommodate two tank locomotives. The ash truck stood up against the stop blocks outside. Inside the shed was the oil and cotton waste store and the carriage cleaner's long box. There was a very old GWR notice with loco shed instructions 'by order of the general manager'. Outside the shed itself was a small cabin with seat lockers. These could seat eight people and there was a long wooden table, a desk with two telephones and a coal-fired stove. Near the shed was a pit for oiling and maintenance under the engines or coaches, and a coal stage, which was only used if there was no delivery of coal from Bath Road depot[12].

[12] Coal for Yatton was usually delivered in an open truck from Bristol and had to be shovelled into loco bunkers by hand.

Yatton engine shed on 24ʰ May 1953 with the Clevedon engine, a 4574 class 2-6-2T no. 5527 built in Swindon in 1928. Photo: R C Riley, (Transport Treasury)

From the memory point of view it is interesting that every time I was told about the number of men working at Yatton station, it seemed to be a different number! It could be that the numbers did change during the different periods covered but I can't be sure of the correctness of Colin Forse's claim that in 1949 at Yatton there were six drivers, six firemen and a cleaner, a chargehand cleaner, plus two shed men – one of whom was Ernest Forse, Colin's father. As it became second nature over a lifetime, I can be sure of the following detailed account of the behind-the-scenes work to prepare the trains for running.

The shed men were not spared an early start. They were on duty at 3 am to prepare the class 14xx auto loco for the Clevedon service. Both Clevedon and Wells locos (class 55x and later 41xxx and 46xxx Ivatt type) had to be prepared and be off the shed by 3.45 am. Before 1963 by 4.40 am the Blagdon service would also have to be ready to leave the shed. Each of these engines took 45 minutes to prepare and could only leave the shed after the signalman had been phoned. The engines would then stand behind the signal box on the up relief line and wait for the shunter.

The Clevedon engine for the 5.30 am service had to be ready to go and join the two coaches in the bay line. It was a mixed train with freight from Bristol West Depot which had been put off at Yatton for Clevedon. Once at Clevedon the goods vans were shunted to the sidings leaving the coaches, and the train was then ready for the first passenger service to Yatton at 6.35 am, arriving at Yatton seven minutes later. This same train was then shunted off to the Cheddar Valley line where it took on water ready to leave for Wells, Tucker Street, at 6.55 am. This train arrived at Wells at 7.35 am and the loco would run round the coaches and return to Yatton at 8 am. The auto-train, meanwhile, had taken over the Clevedon duties.

The men on the next turn were on duty at 11 am and the shed men would be off to Wells to the engine shed where a loco had to be prepared for the freight train to Westbury. A class 22xx also had to be prepared at Wells for the Bristol freight service. The Yatton crew worked to Axbridge Mondays to Fridays and were then relieved by Bristol men.

The men on the last shift of the day worked a trip to Clevedon and back, then left Yatton at 18.10, going on to Bristol via the Cheddar Valley to Witham, Frome and Radstock, arriving at Bristol Temple Meads at 22.28 hours.

By 1956 the turns had changed but there were 16 trains to Clevedon and 16 trains back, with an extra two trips in both directions on Saturdays.

From 8th August 1960 the Clevedon service was by diesel unit (DMU). The 6.10 am service now went to Shepton Mallet where the crews changed over. When they arrived back in Yatton the loco would go back to the shed for servicing.

After the introduction of DMUs on the Clevedon branch, Yatton shed closed. The steam engines for the Cheddar Valley Line were then worked from Bristol and the Wells shed was put under the control of Barrow Road, Bristol.

Right Away to Clevedon

Once, when I had been on duty 12 hours and I had had enough, I was on the up platform and we were supposed to be going to Clevedon. The train came along the platform and Fred Flowers, the driver, said, *'What are you doing standing there?'* I said, *'I've had enough. Twelve hours I've been here.'* *'No-one's listening to you,'* he said. *'It's only the wind that's blowing. Get up in the engine.'* I reluctantly got up in the cab and the foreman came along: *'Right away to Clevedon, Fred.'* And to my surprise, Fred said, *'No, we're going to the shed.'* And we both went home.

Colin Forse

Working Railwaywomen

There wasn't equality for women working on the railway, but some railway wives or daughters found a job on the Strawberry Line – for example, George Stockham's mother worked on the book-stall on Yatton station. Staff shortages due to men going to the war also made some jobs available to women. At Yatton Kath Fear did the

Yatton station staff enjoying a rest in the station garden. From left to right: Jimmy Allen, Frances Chaplin, Kath Fear and Charlie Warburton. Photo by kind permission of Yatton Local History Society.

21

Kath Fear, porter at Yatton station 1942-1967. Photo by kind permission of Yatton Local History Society.

parcels and worked as the goods porter – a job previously done by a man. She started in 1942 and did 25 years service on the station. To get about the station between platforms she used to wheel a trolley over the track-level crossing where planks were laid between the rails. Her son Len became a driver at Yatton.

Two women worked in the Yatton booking office in the 1940s: Frances Chaplin and Dorothy van Klaveram.

Doris Stockham remembered some of the women who worked on the railway at that time. The booking clerk for the Clevedon Flyer was Ann Knott. Bev Green was the manageress and Mrs Mitchell used to look after the waiting room on Yatton station. She got water from one of the steam engines to wash the floors and in the winter she would keep the passengers warm with a lovely fire. Doris also knew the 'porteress' on Clevedon station – Bev Lee.

Because of the munitions supply during the war and the shortage of petrol, there were more train movements and more people in employment on the railway than before or after and all the trains were always full. Reg Bray said there were 30 trains each way to Clevedon during the war and the same service: goods, passengers and specials. There was a mixed goods train at 4 o'clock in the morning and the same in the afternoon to collect the full wagons and vans from Hales Bakery. The empty vans were put in the station and Hales were loading up all day until 4 pm with 10 or 12 tons of cakes to go to small independent shops all over the country.

On the Cheddar Valley Railway the service was the same pre-war and post-war but they were busier during the war. Trains also served the US army camp in Langford: a goods train used to go there two or three times a week loading and unloading materials.

During the war Government Food Stores were set up in the area and because Sandford could not accommodate the extra wagons, goods were unloaded at Congresbury and taken by road by private hauliers to the Old Malt House in Banwell which had been set up as a depot. Sometimes, for example when one thousand tons of sugar arrived, it would take several weeks to clear it.

Reg's War

In 1940 I was called up to the Royal Corps of Signals. Much to my disgust, I was only away three weeks as the railway called me back again. I didn't want to come back but it was apparently a mistake and I shouldn't have been called up in the first place. The Inspector thought he was doing me a good turn by requesting my return. He was mistaken. I was only 21 and I wanted to go in the army as I thought it would be more exciting.

Instead I worked on the railway and joined the Home Guard and the Fire Service. I worked in the Fire Service once a week from 11 am – 7 pm and earned three shillings (15p) for that. Because of this work I was awarded an extra 4 ounce[13] cheese ration per week. We couldn't get to the British Restaurants[14] so we just got quarter of pound of cheese extra.

Reg Bray

---

[13] 125 grams. Some food was strictly rationed in the war.
[14] Restaurants set up to provide cheap nutritious food for factory workers and other workers in the war.

CHAPTER FOUR

Spick and Span

Ron Oddy said, '*The stations on the Cheddar Valley line were all spick and span and always looked clean because the porters and signalmen did it in their own time keeping it nice and tidy. I thought the prettiest little station on the Strawberry Line was Cheddar. It was a beautiful station and in the 1940s, 50s and 60s it still had its impressive Brunel roof of iron and glass. The refreshment rooms had lovely cases of pike that had been caught out of the reservoir.*'

In the lull between trains the station staff were kept busy polishing, dusting, cleaning, tidying and weeding the gardens. The certificates awarded by GWR for the annual station garden competition were highly prized and displayed with pride for the passengers to see. The edge of the platforms were lined with white paint, and if dirty footprints appeared, someone would get the job of touching it up.

The signal box at Congresbury was always kept in beautiful condition by the signalmen who worked there. It was well known that railwaymen weren't allowed in unless they wiped their feet. The waiting room was kept well too; the station master wouldn't allow the staff in there unless they had dusters over their shoes in order to buff up the polished wooden floor.

Standards didn't slip even in wartime, in spite of staff shortages, because the men took a pride in the job and in their place of work.

Doris Stockham remembered Yatton station in 1945:

When people got off the train in 1945 the garden was beautiful. The railwaymen kept the garden nice in their own spare time. There was a bird table and a birdbath and steps to go up off the platform and sit in the garden. YATTON was written in stones. There was a canopy over the footbridge then and a book stall selling papers. You never got wet in the station; it was all covered, even the platforms for the Cheddar Valley Railway and Clevedon branches. It was always spick and span.

When Reg Bray went to Yatton as assistant line man in 1938, one of the foremen was Bill Watts and he was very fond of the garden. In 1938 Yatton station was awarded a monetary prize for the garden. Bill bought young trees: Irish yews, from the GWR nurseries, and planted them. He used to do the garden in his own time, as did Bill Stockham. He became the main gardener after Bill Watts went to Stapleton Road as an Inspector, but others pulled up weeds if they saw them.

Reg said that after the war the garden won several prizes in the Great Western Railway competitions. There were certificates in

Yatton station garden 24th May 1953, showing the young Irish yew trees, the stone edging and ELIZABETH written in stones in celebration of the Queen's Coronation. Photo: R C Riley, (Transport Treasury).

large, medium and small station categories. Yatton was a medium size station and often won certificates. In the summer the station had hanging baskets under the station roof and looked lovely. For the Coronation in 1953 Bill Stockham wrote Elizabeth in stones.

Grass on the sides of cuttings and embankments was kept cut to avoid the risk of fire from cinders. All the drains along the track were checked regularly so they could be kept clear of blockages which might cause flooding. Overhanging trees were cut back and hedges trimmed.

Reg Bray said, 'You could walk up and down the line and never see a weed. Ted Palmer the ganger would pick up any weeds he saw on his way home. The men were proud of the railway and interested in keeping everything looking nice. It was no hardship to them to pick up a weed. It was second-nature.'

All the stations on the Cheddar Valley line were similarly beautifully kept. William Cockram the station master always attended to the station garden at Congresbury. The station was very pretty in the summer with hanging baskets and flower

57xx class 0-6-0 pannier tank no. 9612 draws into Lodge Hill station in April 1955. The trackside garden can be seen on the right. Photo by kind permission of Mike Horwood.

borders on the platform. The stations along the line had all received from Sandford Quarry a gift of Mendip stone with quartz crystals and many of those stones were used to edge flower borders on the station platforms, as at Congresbury, or on the embankment, as seen in the photo taken at Lodge Hill. These crystalline stones can still be seen in the garden at Yatton station.

Keeping Congresbury Clean

When the 2.52 from Yatton was due, Mr Westcott the station master used to come out with all his uniform on and his pill-box hat. There was nobody on the train, nobody at all, but from his bearing you would think the royal train was appearing. He would go on down to Witham on this train. The next train up was the 8 o'clock from Wells so the Congresbury porter working the 'late turn' had from 3 o'clock in the afternoon until 9 o'clock at night with no trains to deal with. He would do all the cleaning then: scrub the waiting room floor, clean the windows, polish the brass, all that kind of thing. In the waiting room there was a large copper oil lamp which was a beautiful thing – unless you were the one polishing it.

Arthur Cockram

All In A Day's Work

Colin Forse recalled vividly the work of a fireman as he had spent thirteen years as a fireman on steam locomotives before promotion to driver. Setting off for work he would be sure to have soap and towel, tea can, sandwiches, sugar, tea tin, rule book and a replacement glass for the water gauge because they sometimes broke on the journey. Colin liked to work the early turns so it was not unusual for him to be booking on duty at three or four o'clock in the morning. Once he had booked on he would need to go to the lamp room and get the tools and headlamps, then proceed to the engine for the first running and prepare it for work. The driver would be making his own arrangements at the same time but the job of the fireman was to check that the handbrake was on, check the water in the boiler, check the fusible plugs, the brick arch and the tube face, and check that no water was leaking from the tubes and stays.

All being well, the fireman would then push what fire had been left in the engine over the grate. He would open up the smoke box and again check for any leaks, closing the door again good and tight. The frame below would then be cleaned of any ashes, the headlamps put on and the sand boxes re-filled as necessary. Now the fireman could go back to the footplate and make up the fire by gradually putting more coal on. The fireman would also trim the coal in the coal-bunker if the pieces were too large. Time was moving on and only 45 minutes was allowed for this preparation (one hour for larger locomotives for mainline operation) so Colin would quickly make the cab presentable by cleaning the pipework and the whole cab environment.

By this time the boiler was coming to full pressure and both injectors needed to be checked to make sure they were working properly. Now the pipe could be used to provide water to wash the floor of the footplate and get rid of all the small dusty coal and also to fill a bucket for the driver and fireman to use to wash their hands.

When the loco was buffered up, Colin would climb down between the loco and carriage to couple up the vacuum and steam heating pipes, then climb back up onto the footplate. The driver and guard would test the brakes and on a goods train the guard would tell the driver the weight of the load, or confirm any temporary speed restrictions. It was then time for the fireman to start the work of maintaining a good boiler pressure and good water levels in the boiler.

On the run it was important to give the driver the power he needed so a fireman learnt by experience exactly where to place a few shovels of coal when the gradient was slightly increasing. The exhaust injector would be turned off as the train reached the end of its journey and the live steam injector gradually increased the level in the boiler and knocked back the steam pressure. This brought the engine gently to rest at its destination and the fireman could then wash his hands, make a can of tea and eat a sandwich before turning the engine round and starting all over again.

The Tide Comes In at Yatton

I was talking to Len Hazell in the signal box one day and was told, *'It isn't the same time every day but on different times of the day and week the signals and lock bars start pulling hard. It's when the tide comes in at Clevedon.'* This wasn't the first time he had complained about this.

We took it seriously every time and the line men would go and have a look at the signals and lock bars but they could never find anything wrong so they used to report back that the signalman was complaining about nothing at all.

Then in 1938 it was decided to update the signalling system between Yatton West and South Liberty signal box on the outskirts of Bristol, so I duly mentioned it to one of the men who had come down from Reading to inspect the system. I told him that there had been a lot of complaints about points and lock bars working hard when the tide was in at Clevedon.

I was very surprised when they took it seriously. The following week some testing gear was brought down and they found that all the rodding and compensators used to lift as the tide was coming in. It was a minute movement – too small to see, but it was enough to make all the pins and joints tight. They proved that because of the marshy ground between Clevedon and Yatton, the tide did make a difference and it did lift the signalling apparatus.

A few days later the wires carrying electricity from Claverham to Clevedon across the moors were renewed. On one day as far as the eye could see there was a new row of electric light poles with the wires suspended between them. The next morning every pole was lying on the ground. That was due to the movement of the ground with the tide. They had to put up two poles side by side and stays across. That was the power of the tide on Yatton.

Reg Bray

29

CHAPTER FIVE

Tokens

When the line was single track, trains had to be limited to one at a time over the various sections between signal boxes. The system devised in the nineteenth century was still in use in the middle of the twentieth. If a token was taken out at Yatton for a down train then another token could not be taken out of another instrument until that train had gone through the section and the token had been replaced in the instrument. A 'token' was a key that fitted into a machine in the signal box. It was about a foot long and made of metal with a handle like a hoop. The token gave the train the right or authority to be on the line and it was handed out through the signal box window to the fireman or driver as the train went slowly by (or by the signalman standing out on the track side). The driver or fireman would then hand the token in at the next signal box, exchanging it for a new one for the next section of line.

Congresbury station was one of these change-over points for tokens because two trains could pass in the station there, but from Congresbury to Axbridge, and from Congresbury to Yatton, it was only single track. Because it so happened there were 13 down trains and 14 up trains, there was an agglomeration of tokens at the Yatton end. Once every ten days the linesman would have to take those tokens out and get them sent down to the other end of the section at Congresbury.

Both instruments had to contain an even number of tokens and it was impossible to put the wrong token into the instrument. They were all phased so Yatton and Congresbury was one phase, Congresbury and Sandford used a different key – it was a different size altogether – and actually up until the 1950s it wasn't a token but a long rod, a staff.

A Heated Exchange

At Cheddar there was a particular relief signalman who didn't change the tokens very well. He would see the fireman leaning out of the cab and he would hold out the token to be changed, and although the engine might only be going at 5-10 mph, he had a nasty habit of moving the token at the last minute and it would go bouncing up the outstretched arm of the poor fireman. One local fireman suffered this for weeks and his arm was black and blue, so finally on one of his morning turns he hung the token on the steam handle all the way, and by the time the train got to Cheddar it had got very warm. That particular signalman might have been a bit more careful after that!

Colin Forse

The Human Token

After the Cheddar Valley line was closed to passengers in 1963, the line remained open for freight to Cheddar from Yatton. A system called 'pilot working' was used because the signal boxes were closed. A relief signalman had to accompany each train from Yatton, or from Congresbury to Cheddar acting as the authority to use the line instead of a token. This relief signalman was, in fact, a human token and the driver's only authority to go onto the single line. A relief signalman would go down to Cheddar with the freight then work in the signal box there, or at Sandford if required. That was the way the line was worked until it closed entirely in 1969.

Other Services at the Station

People used to go to the station when they wanted to send a parcel. I'm talking about the time before Congresbury had a post office. We had a country lorry which delivered to all the outlying areas within a reasonable distance. Parcels going further went on the train. In 1937 all the general goods, the small parcels and small goods traffic was concentrated off the Wrington Vale Line into Congresbury and the Wrington Vale Line virtually only took full truck loads which were delivered by the Congresbury lorry. Its registration was CLR 892. I can't remember what happened yesterday but I remember that! And the railway number was 3224 but I suppose I wrote it so often on delivery sheets it got impressed into me. Writing that number on delivery sheets was one of my duties.

Congresbury was also a telegraph office in the early days before a post office was opened in the village. People could go to the station and send a telegram. It was sent by means of a single needle instrument in the signal box which was a bar Morse code and the needle touched the different sound tin plates. The letter A was left-right, that sort of thing. The telegraph office was just along the verandah. There was an enamel sign saying *Telegraph Office*.

Alan Staddon

When Congresbury station got a truck of goods in early, it fell to Alan Staddon to get the delivery sheets made out. The parcels to be delivered had to be sheeted separately and in the meantime the goods train to Wrington or Blagdon came in and he had shunting to do in the yard so there wasn't much spare time. The stationmaster Mr Cockram used to come out early and he would see to some of the trains while Alan was doing the shunting. Anything that was going away that morning would be put ready and the Blagdon goods train would pick it up on its return journey.

There used to be a travelling safe that was dispatched on the 8.05 Congresbury – Westbury train picking up the receipts from all the stations on the Cheddar Valley line. Every station put the cash that they were remitting to the cashier in a leather pouch and put it in this safe. It was designed so you could drop it in but not get it out. The safe used to go right up the line and come back again in the afternoon.

Complicated Accountancy

There were opportunities to learn accountancy on the railway. It was quite a complicated set up when you realise that an invoice that applied to perhaps only one parcel from Manchester to Congresbury had gone over two railway systems: LMS and GWR, but the carriage charges had to be apportioned – what we called abstracted. That was settled in what was called the Railway Clearing House. Even passenger tickets that ran onto another railway had to be abstracted so Accounts could take the proportion for whatever railway company was due for that part. I got some certificates for railway accountancy.

Alan Staddon

CHAPTER SIX

Special Occasions

A Right Royal Job

A young man worked on the railway at Weston-super-Mare during the Second World War. He was a 'runner', a messenger, whose job it was to run errands and take messages wherever required.
One day at the height of the war he was summoned to the station master's office and told: *'Put your best uniform on and go to Yatton station straight away.'* He got washed and changed and grabbed his pedal bike. He cycled from Weston-super-Mare; the ten-mile ride giving him plenty of time to wonder what he was going to be wanted for at Yatton. When he arrived at Yatton station he reported to the station master's office, rubbing his dusty shoes on the back of his trousers and straightening his tie.

'We want a confidential word with you. The royal train is stabling on the Cheddar Valley branch line tonight,' said the stationmaster.

There were air raids in Bristol at the time. In the early part of 1941 there were 77 air raids in five months, killing 1299 people. The King and Queen were touring the West Country to raise morale but they could not be exposed to the danger in Bristol. Yatton was considered a safe distance. The runner said, *'What do you want me to do?'*

He was told to take the London evening papers down to the royal train when the train carrying them arrived at Yatton. There wasn't long to wait and he duly picked up the newspapers from the guard, went down to the royal train and knocked on the door. The King and Queen were on board so he didn't knock too loudly but a footman in his gold braided uniform opened the door, took the papers and asked, *'Have you eaten tonight? The King and*

Queen will be going to bed in a moment. Come back in an hour and I'll give you some dinner.'

The runner couldn't miss that. He went down an hour later and he had Game Soup, Duck in Orange Sauce and Strawberries and Cream. When he went back to Weston-super-Mare the next day, he said to his mates, *'I've never eaten so well in all my life.'* He kept saying that too, all his life, right up to his dying day!

This story was told by the runner's son at the Strawberry Special in June 2000.

Specials

There were some special trains that the Cheddar Valley line railwaymen particularly remembered. For example, there was a special train service put on for the man who walked across the Gorge in 1961 on a tightrope[15]. Alan Staddon said the Cheddar Valley line had never seen so many people.

The Cheddar Valley line used to be a shortcut to Weymouth in the summer months when the steamers on the south coast were railway owned, and from Weymouth they used to run excursions at weekends. People could go from Bristol to Boulogne for 19 shillings return. That train used to run say once a month on a Sunday morning. It would run down through Yatton about two in the morning, go down to Weymouth, passengers would catch the boat over to Boulogne, come back Monday morning about 3 o'clock.

Arthur Cockram and Allan Staddon both remembered Bertram Mills circus trains. The circus went to Wells and they had their own three trains with special rolling stock for the animals. At night when the circus finished, the trains had to be moved from Wells and take them to Bridgwater. That meant they had to go up to Bristol, run

---

[15] Czech born circus performer Rudi Omankowski did it blindfold and without a safety net. He had done it in 1959 and he repeated it in 1961 on August Bank Holiday. In 1959 a 400 feet cable (a ship's cable from Avonmouth) was used and although they had cleaned it, as it was a hot day it was oozing grease and Rudi had to keep wiping it off.

the loco round the train and go back down the mainline. The line used to be kept open all night for that purpose. A bank engine had to be put on at Axbridge to get the trains up Shute Shelve to Sandford. Not surprising if you consider a cargo of elephants and tigers!

One of the big contracts handled by Congresbury was when there was a delivery of 200,000 tons of aluminium ingots for storage at Cleeve[16]. That kept the lorry drivers busy!

Losing Money on the Horses

Captain Wills at Blagdon (Wrington Vale Line) owned some racehorses and in the summer months they used to have to go to stud. The normal freight train used to bring the horses into Yatton and then they were conveyed up behind the passenger train. When they came back at night, a special train had to be formed to take the horsebox back to Blagdon because there was no regular service at night. And yours truly used to get on board and have a lift up there for the evening. It was after 10 o'clock at night. It was quite frequent that they used to run that train and they lost money on every one. They were bound to lose money because they had to wait till the last train from the Cheddar Valley Line came in after 9 o'clock and had its coaches put away. They also had to wait for a train from Newton Abbot to come with the parcel traffic off the Cheddar Valley before they could run that special. It was late at night before they could run the horse box and a brake van up to Blagdon.

Recorded at the Strawberry Special 2000

Railway staff from Congresbury used to be sent up to Wrington to hold the red flag at the crossing. When specials ran they would get off the train and hold the red flag at the Brinsea crossing (near Poplar Farm) in case of road traffic on a Sunday and then the train would go on to Burrington.

[16] There was a large War Department warehouse where Rhodyate Garage used to be on the main road to Bristol (now housing).

In earlier times on a Sunday in the summer there used to be the Rock of Ages Special. That train would come out from Bristol to Burrington, a double header, and it always used to be packed. They had an outdoor church service there once a year. It was really packed before the war[17]. It was because the curate of Blagdon, Augustus Toplady, had sheltered under a rock in Burrington Combe and was inspired in 1776 to write the famous hymn, Rock of Ages.

Another 'special' was run to take a whole farm from Maidenhead to Blagdon in 1948. This was unusual even in those days and drew interest from the press, especially because the cows had to be unloaded and milked on the platform!

In 1957 the Railway Correspondence and Travel Society (RCTS) ran a special up the Wrington Vale branch.

Wrington station on 28th April 1957 (it had been closed to passengers since 1931) with a platform full of enthusiasts from the Railway Correspondence and Travel Society (RCTS) chartered special. The train was hauled by a pair of ex LMS 2-6-2T engines, nos. 41202 and 41203. Photo: R C Riley, (Transport Treasury).

[17] In 1931 there were said to be 30,000 people attending the open-air service.

CHAPTER SEVEN

Health and Safety

Work on the railway had always been dangerous. Shunters were most at risk because they were often working in railway yards during the hours of darkness, but anyone on the railway might meet with an accident if he let his concentration slip. There were also incidents arising from adolescents larking about at work – and sometimes full-grown men!

Fun 1930s style!

They used to have booking boys working in the signal box putting the train movements in a book. They were only lads of 15 or 16. One said, '*I dropped something under the frame – would you have a look?*' I said, '*I can't see it. Which lever?*' and he said, '*Lever so and so.*' I got down to look at it. He pulled the lever and he had put a detonator under it. It went off like a thousand pound bomb and fragments flew off everywhere. I've still got the scar where shrapnel caught me in the face after 62 years. But it was all done in fun. He didn't realise the consequences.

Reg Bray

Flood Risk at Congresbury

The line from Yatton to Congresbury was nearly level and ran on an embankment. Congresbury station was only 15 feet above mean sea level and the line didn't really rise much until towards Sandford, when it suddenly went up to a 1 in 100 incline. It doesn't sound much but it could cause problems for drivers coming the other way. They sometimes ran pretty fast into Congresbury, once or twice overshooting the platform.

There was a double arm signal which allowed the down trains to come into the usual platform, or the train could be diverted onto the other line. On the other (northern) side of the road bridge[18] there was another steel bridge which crossed the River Yeo. The railway never got flooded. Provision had been made that in the event of serious flooding the water would flow into a huge dip on the Yatton side. Any flood water used to run back over the fields on the Yatton side and not touch the railway at all.

A freight wagon was once derailed on the river bridge. A buffer dropped down into the girder work and that derailed a couple of wagons and stopped everything for a while. But even then the railway didn't close down, not like they would today. The wagon dropped eight or ten inches; two wheels on one side dropped off the rails and it went over the side.

Rocket Ron

It was just after New Year 1963 when I first encountered the snow. I had been asked to work the Wells goods run, which meant a very early start. I went to work about 9.30 in the evening as the weather was snowy, although I wasn't on duty until 2.30 am. There weren't many young drivers who were passed to drive on that route and the older drivers who did know it were on mainline routes. I knew the road to Wells and that run suited me in a way because when we got to Yatton I got off and didn't go back into Bristol.

So, with some difficulty through the snow we made it to Wells in our Class 22xx. We put the engine on shed at Wells and as we were doing so, a bloke from Athelney passed us running. A fireman from another train was chasing a man down the line and told us that we had run over him. He had been pushing his motorbike along the 'four foot'[19] in the pitch black dark. We hadn't even seen him. The fireman caught up with him and made him return to the station. The doctor was called and said there

---

[18] A humped back road bridge took the A370 over the railway

[19] The 'four foot' was the space between the two sets of tracks. On the Cheddar Valley line it was wider than four feet because the railway was originally Brunel's broad gauge.

was no damage to him or his motorbike. He was lucky that night but he was known as Rocket Ron and took risks. In the end he was killed in a motorbike accident.

Colin Forse

Wells Tucker Street, Yatton platform 28ᵗʰ May 1958. Photo: Leslie Freeman, (Transport Treasury).

A Doubly Memorable Day

Alongside the railway was the old sewerage plant. Yatton was growing and needed bigger sewer pipes. The pipes went under the line so we had to be there to dig up the line. A firm from Bedminster was laying the sewerage pipes and the foreman came along late in the afternoon and gave us all a ten-shilling note. That was a lot of money in those days. I was chatting to him about his work and he said, *'We go anywhere over the country working. The next job is right down country. I'm divorced now. Being away from home such a lot causes friction in the home. I haven't seen my wife for seven years. I don't know how she is or where she is living.'* The trains were going very slowly through the works where the pipe was being laid and as he was talking he looked up at a particular train – there was his wife! It was very strange and I never forgot it.

That same day a chappie was working in the permanent way. There's a house down the lane at Wemberham. He said, *'Down there, a mile down the lane, see that house, I shall be living there. I'm getting married next Saturday and that will be my home.'* I said, *'All the best then.'* But I never saw him again.

The next morning I heard that he'd been knocked down and killed. There used to be four lines between Yatton and Hewish. The work had finished for the day and the train should have gone down the mainline but a signalman had let it go down the relief line because he thought the work had finished. The young man who was going to be married was pushing his bike along the relief line and he got killed.

Another day a chap rang from Nailsea signal box. He was coming down with a box of mushrooms for me. I said, 'Right, I'll come up to Yatton East to meet you.' I got to Yatton East but he never turned up. On the way to Yatton both he and his mate were killed by a train. They had been walking along the track on the same line as the trains. They would have been all right if they had been walking on the path alongside the track. At that time you could ride a bike from Penzance to Paddington on the path alongside the track. It was kept tidy and clear.

Reg Bray

Memories of Bristol – Wells

The first train of the day began its journey at Bristol West goods yard, carrying general goods and coal for any stop to Wells. The Bristol driver and fireman would get the engine ready over at St Philips Marsh, go to West Depot and then go on down the mainline. On arrival at Yatton, goods and coal for Clevedon and Yatton were shunted off and the train went on to Congresbury to put off the Blagdon traffic. In 1950 this included goods for Wrington, Langford, Burrington and Blagdon, all the stations on the Wrington Vale line. The loco was serviced with clean water and a top-up of coal, and left for the Yatton men who would arrive later to prepare the engine to work back to Bristol. The Bristol men would go back to Bristol as passengers on a passenger train.

The early Wells goods train would be taken up the bank onto the loop line to wait for the opening of the Congresbury signal box. It fell to the Yatton booking boy to take the token to the driver of this train as it was waiting in the Cheddar Valley line loop and the token could only be obtained once the Congresbury signal box was open. Normally the practice was on any single track line that if the signal box had been closed overnight, then a freight train always had to transfer stock over that single line in the first place[20].

The booking boy would take the token over to the train and the driver would set off straight away. The boy then had the unenviable job of walking back to the signal box in the pitch black with the goods train accelerating right beside him.

All the stations to Wells were serviced every day including Saturdays. The passenger services started from Yatton and Wells at almost the same time – Yatton at 6.50 am and from Wells at 7 am, crossing one another at Cheddar. Throughout the day there was a good service until the last train from Wells left for Yatton at 8.15 pm Monday to Saturday. The Sunday service was only one train in each direction. From Wells there was also a freight turn to Witham and return which serviced Shepton Mallet and Cranmore as well.

[20] This was for safety reasons to check the line before putting passenger trains onto it.

An Ivatt 2MT 2-6-0 leaves Lodge Hill station for Wells tender first on 1st April 1955. Photo by kind permission of Mike Horwood.

45xx class no. 4572 pulls out of Lodge Hill on 12 July 1955 . Photo by kind permission of Mike Horwood.

Axbridge to Wells without a Fireman

I was a fireman with a driver named Fred Flowers and we weren't getting on very well – and neither was the engine because you really needed to work as a team to get the best out of a steam engine. So when we arrived at Axbridge going south, the driver said, *'Get off.'* I got off because he was getting on my nerves. The signalman gave him the token and off he went.

Mr Greenham, the station master, who was watching, said, *'You missed the train!'* I said, *'No, I didn't miss the train. The driver chucked me off.'* He frowned. *'Oh well, go over in my office. You'd better have a cup of tea and get back on the train when it comes back.'* So I had my tea and the train came back from Wells and Fred barked, *'Get back on'.* I said, *'No, you went to Wells on your own, you can go to Yatton on your own.'* *'Get up here,'* he said. I thought it had gone far enough, so I did. But he wanted me to know that he had won the argument, so he said, *'Before we move, who said this little engine couldn't go to Wells and back without you? It went to Wells and back, so what's your problem now?'* So I said, *'Well, you took the chance, driver, it was entirely up to you. You're in charge.'* He said, *'You know this is a reporting matter, don't you?'* I said, *'Well, if you report me, you'll get reported for going to Wells without a fireman.'*

Anyway we went off. When you used to run downhill from Winscombe to Sandford and Congresbury you would expect plenty of water to be in the boiler and I didn't think there was enough. Fred was an experienced driver and he said, *'You have to have confidence in what you're doing. I knew I could get to Wells and back firing and driving. I wouldn't have done it if I hadn't been sure I could get away with it. Learn the lesson.'* He told me, *'If you have to stand on the bucket to look down in the water gauge to see if there's any water in it, then you've had it.'* He was right and I did learn that lesson from him. Anyway, we were the best of pals after that.

Colin Forse

Empty wagons that originated in Weston super Mare used to be picked up from Yatton, and pushed up to the quarry at Sandford.

Ivatt Class 2 2-6-2T 41202 pulls into Lodge Hill station on 11th April 1955.
Photo by kind permission of Mike Horwood.

The little auto engine used for this job was the second engine at Yatton, a Class 41[21]. It was quite a sharp incline to get into the quarry sidings and the wagons would need to be pushed over the Sandford-Winscombe road. It was an almighty push to get the wagons up the incline and then it required two men taking a lot of care to make sure not to push the wagons straight across the Somerset County Council road because they had made it clear that they didn't like that. It was difficult because although it was a dangerous practice to cross the road, the train had to be going fast – 15-20 mph – to push those wooden wagons up into the quarry.

You Want Smoke, I'll Give You Smoke

One Sunday the famous Ivo Peters and Norman Locket appeared at the station to take photos of the Clevedon engine no. 1463. Fred Flowers was on duty and they asked him if he could make smoke for them to improve their photos. To this day it remains unknown what went into the firebox, but they made smoke all right! The branch line was blacked out for nearly an hour!

Colin Forse

[21] This was an Ivatt Class 2 2-6-2 tank engine.

CHAPTER EIGHT

Tricks and Treats

Begorrah!

One day two Irish Catholic priests came into Yatton station to book tickets to Ireland for the following day. Herbie Wilcox the shunter happened to be around when they came, and he liked a laugh. The priests had their suitcases with them and once they had got their tickets they asked if they could leave their cases there while they went off somewhere. Herbie said he would put them in the parcels office which was on the upside platform of the station. Herbie couldn't resist having a look to see what was in the cases and he opened one. Inside was a priest's regalia – everything connected with the life of a priest.

Every evening Mr Ralph the stationmaster used to walk down from his house at the top of Station Approach because he liked a bit of company and he liked to chat with the staff and passengers. On this particular evening he entered into conversation with a vaguely familiar Irish priest and it was some time before he realised that it was Herbie, dressed up and trying out his best Irish accent.

Reg Bray

Fish and Chips in Clevedon

Colin Forse said that on Fridays the fish and chip shop in the Triangle at Clevedon received boxes of fish by rail. Mr Webb, the owner, said that if his boxes of fish were delivered to him unbroken, he would give the train crew free fish and chips. That was a nice treat, free fish and chips on a Friday, so they took care to handle the boxes very carefully.

Egg and Bacon at Blagdon

The Blagdon branch from Congresbury to Blagdon served Wrington, Langford, Burrington and then Blagdon. In the days when the beam engine was working, they used to take coal traffic from Yatton to the Blagdon Waterworks' special siding. One driver, Len Fear, had an auntie living just outside Langford station, so when he was driving the Blagdon goods train he would get out at Langford and go to Auntie's for eggs and bacon. The fireman, whose name was Brian, would do the work. He would go on to Blagdon, offload the coal and then come back to Langford for Len and he would get back in the cab. Len's mother was a porter at Yatton: Kath Fear. I'm talking about 60 years ago now. It's hard to remember.

Reg Bray

Onions in their Jackets, Eggs on the Shovel

Ron Oddy remembered bacon and eggs from the shovel with Charlie Nelms and sometimes cooking onions in their jackets and kippers on the train. It all tasted better then!

Cold Beef at Cheddar

On Wednesdays Cheddar had a sort of market day, and in the 1950s a lady owned a restaurant there and it was very popular with farmers and traders who used to go in and have their lunch. When the train came back up with the Wells goods train, if there was any beef left over, she used to go over to the station and take the engine driver, fireman and guard left-over slices of beef. The men really looked forward to their market day treat. They were pleased that she never asked for any money but then she probably wouldn't have got any anyway!

Spuds, You Like?

Mr Dennis Clements, who was in charge of the yard at Wrington, told me he had bought a load of potatoes and he had been surprised to get five loads instead of four and he said to me, *'Do you want some potatoes?'* I said, *'Yes, please,'* so he said, *'Give me £5 for them'.* I said it was far too much. I thought I was buying a bag of potatoes. He said, *'No, not a bag, a vanload.'* So I bought a vanload of potatoes and had to get them down to Yatton.

The guard said, *'I'll put a label on: Yatton – Local Sticks.'* The sticks were firelighters made of pieces of wood. We loaded the potatoes, duly shunted into the cove and when we opened the bags we'd been done. They were blue. They had been dyed. They were all right to eat though. But I thought, *'What am I going to do with a vanload of blue potatoes?'* One of my acquaintances said, *'Why don't you take them up to Bristol and sell them to the men there?'* There were plenty of people up there who would like blue potatoes but how could I get a van load of potatoes up to Bristol? A friend said, *'I'll ring the boss up for you.'* The boss said, *'Yes, I don't mind a bag of potatoes being delivered.'* But he didn't realise we were talking about a vanload! My friend agreed for the van to be labelled *Empty to Bristol Bath Road.* And it went to St Philips Marsh and was put off there, and then the local train took it down to Bath Road shed, next to the lamp house. They opened up the doors and there was a van load of potatoes in bags at a bargain price, payable to me. Everyone in Bath Road depot went home with a bag of blue potatoes!

Colin Forse

Pick Your Own at Yatton

I had an allotment on the bit of land between the Cheddar Valley Railway and the mainline. There were about a dozen allotments there, mostly rented to railwaymen. I grew gooseberries, strawberries, carrots, onions, cauliflowers, everything. One day I was down there at the same time as Fred Flowers, one of the drivers – he was a notability in Yatton. He was a wonderful gardener. All his produce was exceptional. He was digging his potatoes up. I helped him and because of that he gave me a sack of potatoes to take home. I put the sack on my back and was very glad to take it home with me. A mate of mine came up and he started bagging up potatoes with Fred too. When the job was finished he said, *'Where's my sack then?'* Fred said, *'I never asked you to pick any up!'*

One of the other allotment holders was Dick Harding who kept the Clifton Foot Harriers. He had a plot that was 200 yards by 6 yards. He grew beautiful vegetables. Another chap, Herbie Allan, used to get the ashes from the gasworks to put on the gardens because it was wonderful fertiliser and they grew excellent fruit and vegetables too.

Reg Bray

Making the Connection

The Clevedon train connected to 31 trains a day. The only train that it didn't connect with was the stopping train, the 5.35 Bristol – Weston train. However, there was one passenger who used to catch the 5.55 train from Clevedon after work. Working to rule and timetable the journey would take seven minutes to Yatton, but with a bit of bribery and a fair wind the train could get there at 6 o'clock. The happy passenger could just manage to dash over the bridge and get his connection.

CHAPTER NINE

Stuck in Snow – the Photographer's Story

In the very hard winter of 1962/3, Mike Horwood, living at Cheddar, became concerned about his parents, who lived in Westbury-sub-Mendip. It had been snowing on and off from Boxing Day into the New Year and the forecast was very bad. Mike wanted to check that they didn't need anything, and as the roads were impassable, he set out to walk there. He took his camera in case he saw anything interesting on the way.

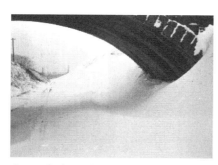

Snow drift under railway bridge. Deep and crisp and not even at all.

Mike knew the snow was often bad at Draycott, but he was still quite surprised when he looked north down the railway track from the station bridge and could see steam from at least two engines stuck in a snow drift.

Mike decided to take a closer look and took a series of photos which appear on the following pages. The film did not get developed and was forgotten and the camera eventually got put in the loft.

Many years later Mike found the old camera in his loft and realised it still had a film in it. He had forgotten entirely what

From the station bridge Mike could see steam trains stuck at the distant signal.

Mike was pleased eventually to make it to Westbury-sub-Mendip.

might be on it but he decided to have it developed. A couple of weeks later, when he told the landlady at the Westbury Inn what he had found on the old film, she asked to borrow the pictures. Next week they appeared in the local paper, much to Mike's surprise!

One of the people who saw the photos was Colin Forse, the driver of one of the engines, and he was very excited to find out that this little piece of local railway history had been captured on film. He told the story of being stuck in the snow many, many times, and the details were sometimes inconsistent, but the version that follows was delivered to a delighted audience in the Chapter House, Yatton, in October 2000, accompanied by some of Mike's photos.

Stuck in Snow – the Engine Driver's Story

On Wednesday 2nd January 1963 at about 2 am I reported to Barrow Road Depot. It had been snowing on and off since Boxing Day, and Control asked me, '*How do you feel about working to Wells?*' I said, '*All right. I'll try.*' '*Will you go as far as you can get?*' '*Yes,*' I said. So I got my fireman, Clive Joslin, and took the light engine 46506 and at 6.30 am we were at Yatton. I said to Clive, '*Let's fill the tender up and go to the signal box and see what's going on.*' When I came back across the crossing I picked up a couple of packing shovels with a sack and put them on the engine. I wanted to be prepared for whatever we were going to meet with. I went over to the shed where my Dad was on duty and borrowed a steam lance.[23] We got the token from the signal box and went on to Congresbury.

The signalman at Congresbury was called Bob Ford, a lovely fellow. It was a bit of a problem changing the points from the Wrington line to the Cheddar line because of the snow, but I used the steam lance to deal with it. Bob then said, '*We've just had a message from Bristol. You've got to wait until an engine comes with a snow plough. They are sending 2277 with an inspector to give*

---

[23] A pipe could be screwed onto the smoke box so steam went straight from the boiler to the lance.

orders.' So we waited at Congresbury and the engine finally arrived and out got the biggest man you've ever seen. He was huge.

Without any introduction he said, *'You've got to couple up behind me and you've got to push me to Cheddar.'* I said, *'Who are you?'* He said, *'I'm Inspector Webb.'* I said, *'Oo-ooh.'* Then more politely I asked, *'What do you want to do guvnor?'* He said, *'Well, we'll go and clear the line with both engines, and see how far we get.'* I said, *'OK.'*

Colin's engine, an Ivatt Class 2 2-6-0 no. 46506, adrift and forlorn in the snow. This locomotive was shedded at St Phillips Marsh, Bristol. It had been built in Swindon in 1952 and was scrapped under the BR modernisation scheme in 1967.

We coupled up behind the snow plough as requested and set off. We went with no problem to Sandford, then Winscombe, where there was a gentleman stood on the platform, believe it or not, in a black coat, umbrella, briefcase and bowler hat. He heard a train coming and he thought he was going to get on it, didn't he? But unfortunately for him it was a snow plough, and he still just stood there on the platform. He never moved. He got covered with snow. My mate Clive said, *'Did you see that? It was the Homepride flour grader!'*

We had no problem all the way to Cheddar. The signalman there said, *'It's bad between Cheddar and Draycott. The morning news said there's a blizzard coming at 12 o'clock. It's going to be a local storm, particularly bad in the Mendip Area.'* Control had also told him that they wanted the inspector to know that I knew the area and could give him local knowledge. He had never been on the Cheddar Valley line before. Anyway, we got the token to Draycott and as I did know the road I said to the Inspector, *'We've got to watch it – when we get up to the distant signal it'll be bad because it blows down off the embankment there.'*

When we finally got up towards a chicken farm about 50 yards from the station, the snow was looking very deep in drifts. The inspector stopped us and said, *'I'll get off and have a look.'* *'Don't do that,'* I said. *'Don't get off.'* *'Why not?'* he said. I said, *'You get off here mate and I don't know how much snow is on top of that ditch.'* *'What ditch?'* he said. *'I can't see any ditch!'*

I had warned him, but he stepped off anyway. I told you he was a big man. The driver and fireman of the snow plough engine stood watching, Clive and I stood watching, and this Inspector disappeared into the snow and all you could see was his brown leather gloves above his head holding up his umbrella. The other driver said, *'Oh, he's gone down in the ditch.'* We both sighed and I said, *'We'll get him out.'*

We got to him quickly but it took all four of us to get him out. I was a bit concerned about him because he needed to dry out. He said, *'How did you know the ditch was there?'* I said, *'In the summer there's always water about just here.'* Well, it was the River Axe. Of course there was water in it!

We then considered moving on. The inspector was keeping close to the fire. He was producing as much steam as the engine. *'We can't go on,'* he said. *'The best thing is for you to go back and then if you get stuck I'll come back as well and pull you out.'* The snow plough was stuck and the snow was high over the front of it. We were stuck behind it and the snow was high over the couplings. It took us over an hour to uncouple so we could go back.

We started off backwards as steadily as we could, but my little engine was near the chicken farm when we parted company from the snow plough engine. We shot off backwards and the snow was at the back end. Well, that was it. We were going nowhere, forwards or back. We were well and truly stuck and so was 2277.

With snow plough, Collett Class 2251 0-6-0 no. 2277 stuck fast in the snow. Colin's engine, 46506, can be seen behind.

Another view of the Collett goods no. 2277. This Swindon built locomotive was scrapped a year later after 30 years' service.

Clive and I walked up to Draycott along the bank. We took a shovel and we needed it because we actually had to dig down with a shovel to find the telephone box and ring up to say we were stuck. Unfortunately the lady in the railway telegraph office wouldn't take the reverse-charges call. She said, *'You'll have to pay.'* *'It's railway business,'* I said. I wasn't going to pay for the call! In the end she said, *'I'll find out,'* and she got the foreman. He accepted the call and asked me, *'Where's the Inspector?'* I said, *'He's sat in the engine, drying out his clothes.'* *'What do you mean, he's drying out?'* I said, *'Well, he went down in nine feet of snow and his feet were in the River Axe.'* He said, *'Well I can't get anyone to come and relieve you now.'* To be honest I wasn't expecting it.

The blizzard came and it really was bad. The Rule Book said that if you couldn't proceed, you had to take the token and walk back to the last signal box that you had passed – Cheddar in this case – to get assistance so a pilotman can come in to assist. The Inspector said, *'That's the fireman's job.'*

I said, *'You can't send him on his own to walk back in a blizzard. You can't send him. I should go with the signalman. He lives in the station house.'*

'No,' he said, *'You're the driver. You can't go. You are responsible for the engine.'*

In the end he decided he would go himself with the signalman and off he went. Not long after he had gone we had a visitor as the lady from the chicken farm sent her boy up to see us. He asked if we could spare a bucket of coal. The four of us sent back the message, *'Yes, if you'll give us a chicken.'* What a deal! We dined on two packets of fig biscuits and a chicken, which we cooked on the fire. Then we built ourselves an igloo of snow to keep out the wind and cold and did our best to sleep.

The Inspector finally came back the next morning with two other railwaymen. He said, *'I've got some bacon, eggs, bread and some black sausage.'* We surprised him when we said we had had something to eat the night before, but we happily cooked the breakfast on the shovel. Clive had been keeping the fire going so we didn't freeze. The inspector said, '*I don't know what's going to happen. There's chaos everywhere.*'

The day passed without much to do except shiver, but we were getting hungry again when somebody came down with a hurricane lamp and said, '*My missus says, Would you like something hot to drink?*' So we said, '*Yes please,*' and the four of us – the drivers and firemen from the two engines – marched up behind him. He had cleared all the snow and made a path so we could get in his house. There was a big farmhouse kitchen with a big table and the farmer's wife had cups and saucers bigger than soup plates. She said, '*Where's the rest of you?*' I said, '*There's only four of us, ma'am!*' She said, '*I just heard on the West of England Home Service that there's a hundred men digging you out.*' She had got enough food there for one hundred men! We learnt afterwards that there was another incident on the Somerset and Dorset Line and that was the one reported on the wireless.

After we had eaten our fill and taken some sandwiches away for later, we thought we might as well go off to the pub. Our engine wouldn't be going anywhere! We spent a bit of time at the pub and got a bit peckish again. I asked for a cheese sandwich. The landlady said, '*I've got plenty of cheese but I've got no bread.*' I said, '*Hang on,*' and I went up to the house next to the station where the lady who had had the coal from us was outside sweeping snow. I asked her, '*Would you like some more coal for your fire?*' She said, '*What's the deal?*' and I said, '*A loaf of bread.*' So the landlady got the bread, we got some sandwiches with our beer and the lady who gave us the bread got another bucket of coal.

We had nowhere else to go at closing time so we went back to the engine where the snow was all piled up around the cab. We made up the fire and with the snow all piled up around us it was warm. We slept there up until about midnight when we woke up because we could hear a diesel and several other engines. They intended to come in and clear the line. I understood that they couldn't just shut the branch, but I didn't know how they hoped to clear the line with the snow as deep as it was. The diesel hydraulic

Hymek 7046 driven by Bill Farr came along through the snow, clearing it as he went, but then he got stuck as well. He was reversing then driving fast forward, battering the snow like a ram, trying to push the snow out of the way, but in the end he had to give up.

Hymek Type 3 diesel hydraulic locomotive no. D7046 comes to the rescue and also gets stuck in snow. Now there were three.

D7046 struggles to get a foothold on the track. This locomotive was barely two years old at this time. It was scrapped in Swindon under a standardisation programme in 1972 with less than ten years' service.

Inspector Webb climbed up to look in the sand boxes[23]. On most engines you could stand on the sand boxes to look in and check the sand contents. He just didn't seem to be in the right place, so I asked Mr Webb, *'Have you got sandboxes on the Hymek?'* He said, *'What do you mean? Come and have a look.'* Then he noticed. *'Oh my God'*, he said, *'he's gone off the rails!'*

What had happened was that the Hymek had been riding up and down on the ice on its sandboxes. The loco was going up and down, up and down, but nobody knew the wheels weren't on the rails. It had been Thursday for a very long time and all Thursday night an engine had been trying to get to us but it never got there. I burst into tears. Then I thought, *'Think of all that overtime.'*

The Bath Road depot breakdown train arrives at Rodney Stoke behind Collett goods locomotive no. 2217.

The next day, Friday morning, the Bath Road breakdown train got to us from the Westbury side. It only just made it because it was still snowing and freezing. The breakdown train came along

[23] Sand was carried so that it could be spread on the rails to improve traction in case of ice.

No. 2217 waits at Rodney Stoke while decisions are made. Built at Swindon in 1940 it will not have a long wait until it is scrapped in 1965.

Team in action preparing to pull the diesel locomotive over re-railing ramps. Chief Inspector Jack Whitney is on the right presiding over the operation.

with a big chain on and the plan was that he would pull the Hymek back onto the rails. In the breakdown train was Chief Inspector Mr Whitney. He was a cockney. I didn't think they ever had snow up there in London because he didn't seem to know what was going on. *'How did you manage for food?'* he said. *'Oh, we were fed like royalty, sir,'* I told him. *'Oh, where did you get food? There's no shop.'* *'No,'* I said, *'but there's a chicken farm.'* *'A chicken farm?'* *'Yeah. A nice lady gave us some eggs and Mr Webb got us some bacon, and I brought some Oxos so we had a hot drink.'* I always had a couple of Oxos and some stale bread on me. That was the plat du jour.

We were soon flattening the snow riding up and down past the place where Mr Webb went in. The other engine finally made it up to the Hymek and they were preparing to pull it back on the rails. We were dead beat and the foreman told us to drop the fire on our loco, get our gear and go home on the other engine. We were relieved at last – and we were very relieved indeed. We had been on duty from 2 am Wednesday until 11.20 am Friday.

Just beyond Draycott in Easton Cutting more engines were stuck. It was the other side of the Bristol area and Westbury was looking after that side.

I was quite ill after being stuck in the snow. I hadn't had much sleep and my legs were very sore because they had been in my Wellington boots so long. The doctor came to see me and said, *'What on earth have you been doing?'* I said I had been on my engine stuck in the snow. She said, *'You could have walked.'* I said, *'I couldn't, I was working!'* She said I needed a rest. I took a rest for six days but there was no company sick pay so that was long enough.

Colin Forse

After a couple of days Mike Horwood, who lived near the market cross in Cheddar, heard the roaring of a diesel engine. As no trains had been running since the incident he had photographed, he went along to the station to see what was making all the noise. In the station was the same Hymek diesel, still covered in snow from its ramming of the snow drifts at Draycott.

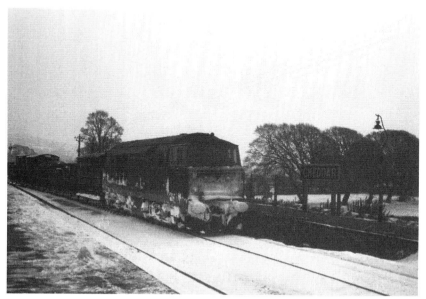

Hymek at Cheddar Station showing the depth of snow encountered in the drift. There had been no thawing since the engines had all been stuck in snow.

Two Type 3 Class 5 diesels – classmates of D7406 – are preserved on the West Somerset Railway. This class was built in the early 1960s and saw less than ten years service before being withdrawn in 1972 and scrapped at Swindon.

CHAPTER TEN

Unhappy Days – Closure

When the branch lines closed most of the railwaymen were devastated. Morale hit rock bottom after years of uncertainty. They realised that trains were not being patronised as they had been and that goods were increasingly being transported by road. Arthur Cockram said that there was no possibility of protest and that when the staff committees were consulted it was obvious that there was nothing to be done – closure was inevitable.

There was no ceremony organised by British Rail but a few local railwaymen and a lot of sympathetic and nostalgic local people made an event of the last scheduled passenger train to run down the line. Colin Forse was in the cab with the driver and fireman, savouring the last trip. The guard was Bernard Still of Weston super Mare. Detonators had been placed along the track and people turned out at the stations along the route to cheer and wave. Most people then returned on the last train the other way – just two coaches crammed to the luggage racks with about 250 passengers.

Discussing the effect of the branch closure on signalling staff, Arthur Cockram said:

'On the Cheddar Valley line alone, everyone lost their jobs. Most took their redundancy and left. Five signalmen in West box at Yatton lost their jobs, three in East box, three at Hewish – that makes eleven. Then there were three at Puxton, three at Claverham so that's 17. There were also three Class 2 men, one Class 1 and two specials. That makes 25 signalmen based under Yatton, without counting all the other staff.'

Arthur Cockram recalled that after the line had closed the Congresbury station buildings were left in situ a long time.

Demolition at Congresbury

I was standing on my allotment down there. I had had a piece of ground down there for years. I could hear all this hammering and I discovered there was a brand new machine down there on the station. J C Moore of Wells was the demolition company. They were there with their brand new machine and they took five hours to knock down the whole of the goods shed and the station buildings. They just picked it all up and dumped it in the pond. All that beautiful stonework, just dumped in the pond.

I went down there with Arthur Westcott, the former station master, one evening. The platform trolleys were still there – the old four wheelers that they used to put the milk churns on – and I said to Arthur, *'Do you want some timber, Arthur?'* and he said, *'Yes, why?'* And I said, *'Come on then, give us a hand.'* We went down to the goods shed. I knew what was there. The roof was completely lined with pine wood. A whole lot of it. And it was lying on the ground. So we went down picking up this wood and in came a fellow with a little truck and he said to me, *'What do you reckon you're up to?'* I said, *'Just gathering this wood.'* He said, *'Who are you and what are you?'* And I said, *'Well, I'm the signalman and this is the station master.'* I said, *'And we're having this wood.'* He said, *'Who gave you permission?'* I said, *'The chap on the machine.'* He said, *'Well, that's all right then, but leave all that long stuff because I want it myself.'*

So we took all these huge long lengths of wooden boards off the top and left them to one side and we just took the smaller ones. The next day they came along with some diesel and set fire to the lot. Burnt the lot, platform and all. There had been a lovely wooden platform in the goods shed. They just set fire to the lot. They were given the job to clear it all up and they laid it all flat.

Arthur Cockram

Arthur Cockram had also made an enquiry as to whether he could buy the station building and convert it into a house. He knew he wasn't the only one. He had a reply to say that his name would be added to the list. Next thing that happened – they pulled it down.

There was a rumour at one time that the Bluebell Line was going to take over the line Yatton to Cheddar. It never came off and the men thought it was a pity it didn't.

Sizing Up the Job

The signals were all destroyed. They had the contractor lift the line from Cheddar to Yatton. I happened to be down at the station on morning after the railway was closed and I saw two fellows with black macs on. I recognised the macs and I saw the men go up the steps to the signal box and when they came down I said, *'Do you want to get in the box? I've got a key.'* 'No, that's all right,' they said. They were just walking through to see what was involved and what they had got to retrieve. One of them said to me, *'We were wondering the best way to get to remove all the rails and recover stuff.'* I said, 'It's quite simple really, isn't it? They then asked, *'How would you do it?'* I said, *'Well, all I would do is to have a train start at Cheddar and come back towards Yatton. Quite simple.'* And that's what they did. They ran a train down every day. They brought the empties in and took the loaded trucks out and there was quite a lot of stuff went somewhere other than where it should have gone – including at Congresbury. They always had a covered van to recover all the telegraph wires to start with. They were copper. When I was working, my Inspector said to me one day, *'I've been trying to get Cheddar on the telephone. I can't get any reply.'* So I took a walk down the line in my own time. I found out the reason. Between Congresbury and Sandford somebody had been taking the telegraph wires down. All the wires disappeared.

Arthur Cockram

One of the drivers had a next-door neighbour whose father had a business in Sandford quarry. He tried his damnedest in the later years when they were talking of shutting the railway, to buy the wagons for the quarry, but they turned him down. He kept asking and they kept turning him down. They were determined they were going to close the railway come hell or high water. So all the arguments anyone could put forward were ignored.

Daylight Robbery

But when they were in Congresbury station on the very last day – I didn't know what happened till some time after, but they used to keep the demolition train there overnight and take it out in the morning, and put another one back in. They had some night workers turn up and empty the contents. Then a fellow came in with a mini van. He was wearing a long dust coat identifiable to the locomotive section of the railway. That fellow filled that van up with all the little wooden keys that used to hold the rails into the chairs. He was retrieving them because they were all branded GWR. He took them in to an Open Day at Bath Road, Bristol and I saw him flogging them in there. Nobody asked where they came from or who he was. He just took what he fancied and whatever he could make some money on from the demolition site and no-one ever questioned him. The railway was robbed right, left and centre.

They didn't want to preserve anything if they could help it. At Chippenham they had a huge brick-built goods shed and the council tried to put an order on it to preserve it but the railway descended on it late on a Saturday night and by Sunday morning it was a heap of bricks. They made sure there was no preservation order put on that one.

Allan Staddon

Reg Bray remembered unhappy days in March 1963 waiting for the Beeching Report to come out in the paper. Railwaymen were no wiser than the general public about which lines were going to close and had to wait to read about in the newspapers. Then when the report did come he wasn't happy about the way it was handled. He was one of the telecommunications staff involved in recovering signal wires. They got notice that from 10 pm the line would be closed, and the very next day they were sent to recover redundant materials.

No Way Back

After the last train had gone down the Cheddar Valley line in 1966 the river bridge over the Yeo at Congresbury was immediately cut with an acetylene welder, directly after the last train had gone over. Straight away. It was a small steel bridge for a single line and they quickly dismantled it immediately so no protest could be made about the closure. The quarry at Sandford made an application to British Railways to have the line reconnected as they found it difficult to transport the stone. They got out prints for re-signalling but when they went into the cost of reinstating the river bridge it was decided it was too expensive. It was a shame.

Reg Bray

Doris Stockham remembered the heartache in Yatton when the Cheddar Valley line closed:

'When the railway closed lots of men were due for retirement. Tudor Gibbons the station master went to the office in Bristol and so did Viv Wathen. Quite a few went to mainline firing or driving to Bristol. Many had done their time and lots left because they didn't like the changes.

A meeting was held at Yatton and we all went to protest. They said they would listen to what we had to say and then come back to us. They said they would start a bus because the line wasn't paying and they would have to shut it down. But we railway people would have concessions on the bus from Yatton to Clevedon and we would have to catch it at Yatton station. The bus ran for 6 or 9

67

months and then they ran the bus no more. So we were no longer able to use the privileges. Everyone was very much up in arms against the closures. They were paying lines. Lots of people lost their jobs, especially on the Clevedon line. Children from Yatton had to leave the Clevedon schools because they couldn't get there. The railway kept saying it wouldn't pay but they had made their minds up and they closed it down.

We rode on the last train to Cheddar from Yatton. We couldn't go down to the station to ride on the last train to Clevedon, George was just too upset. We saw the pictures in the paper. On the ride to Cheddar people were sad, it was cutting us off from Wells and Cheddar. It meant I couldn't go to Congresbury on the train to see my godson – I had to walk instead. He still lived in the house for a while until he could move to Bristol. It meant you had to find a different sort of travel. There were no buses to Wells. It was all a very sad time.'

'I am pleased it's become a cycle path. It's still our Cheddar Valley Line. It's remarkable how it's been cleared from Yatton station. Thanks to everybody who's worked so hard to get it like that. It's absolutely brilliant.'

Doris Stockham (recorded October 2000)

CHAPTER ELEVEN

Find the Strawberry Line ghosts, follow the ghost trail:

The Strawberry Line Society (formerly Cheddar Valley Railway Walk Society)

In 1977 a small group of motivated people in Winscombe set out to secure a traffic free footpath for the community before it became fragmented by piecemeal disposals. In 1978, the Aims and Objectives of the formally constituted Cheddar Valley Railway Walk Society were 'to provide a public route on the former Cheddar Valley line for leisure and recreation and to conserve the land as a nature reserve'.

The Society persuaded the District Council to purchase the seven linear miles within Woodspring District (now North Somerset) before going on to finance and set up the first seven miles of the scheme from Yatton to the A38 at Shute Shelve between 1983 and 1985. Phase two, the Axbridge to Cheddar Cyclepath, followed in 1990, established by the Axbridge/Cheddar Cycleway Branch of the Society in collaboration with Sedgemoor District Council as landowner. This provided a much needed safe cyclepath to school for local pupils avoiding the hazardous A371.

In 1983 the Council would not agree to joint use for cycling on the North Somerset section. With a change of climate in more recent years, a Heritage Lottery Grant was obtained to convert all of the route for cycling and also enhanced heritage, disabled access, interpretation and conservation. The work was carried out between 2004 and 2006. This now forms part of National Cycle Network route 26 Clevedon to Weymouth.

The eleven miles of Strawberry Line is widely recognised as a major artery through the countryside of North Somerset and Somerset Counties for leisure and recreation, heritage, green transport and tourism. Conservation is important. The wide variety of linear landscapes, cuttings, embankments, moors, rhynes, woodland, hills and even a tunnel all contribute to make this, at 74 acres, the largest formally designated Local Nature Reserve within North Somerset.

The Society, now known as the Strawberry Line Society, and its Branches, continues to manage the land in partnership with Local Authorities and other volunteer organisations (YACWAG/Sustrans etc).

Ongoing aims are to link with Clevedon and Blagdon via Wrington and work with other organisations/interest groups to extend the amenity to Wells and beyond where it could potentially form part of an 84 mile 'Somerset Circle' linking with other networks.

The Strawberry Line Association is a federation of the groups involved: www.thestrawberryline.org.uk

Yatton – Strawberry Line Café
The community cafe can be visited in the restored Victorian waiting room (Grade II Listed) on the down platform of Yatton station. The building was sensitively restored in 2009 by a Community Interest Company which trains and employs adults with learning disabilities. It retains its wooden panelling and original doors. Photos and railway memorabilia are on display and a collection of railway books and magazines can be viewed while taking refreshments.
www.strawberrylinecafe.co.uk

Yatton station garden
Volunteers have restored the prize-winning GWR station garden. The Irish yew trees were planted in 1938 when the garden was at its heyday. The station garden project has been running since 2000 and welcomes new volunteers. It was a runner-up in the ACORP

Awards 2015 for a large station garden and has won Neighbourhood Awards in 2013 and 2015 from the Britain in Bloom campaign.

The Railway Inn, formerly the Railway Hotel, is a beautiful stone building contemporary with the railway station. The stationmaster's house was at 1 Station Approach, west of the station.

Bridges over the former Clevedon branch line can be seen in Wemberham Lane and Horsecastle Farm Road.

Congresbury station platforms

There are no station buildings left on the site but the platforms are still there and the cycle and footpath runs between them. The up platform is of local carboniferous limestone from Henley Quarry, Yatton, but the downside platform is built of Rodney Stoke conglomerate, formed 200 million years ago when beds of broken shells mixed with bands of Carboniferous Limestone pebbles on the ancient shoreline when the Mendips were a string of islands. The stationmaster's house is on the east side of the Strawberry Line Heritage Trail. A little further down the Bristol Road towards Weston-super-Mare are two railway cottages which once housed GWR staff employed at the station. The Greek restaurant used to be the Railway Inn.

Wrington Vale Light Railway

A memorial bench has been erected on the site of the junction of the Strawberry Line with the Wrington Vale Light Railway (south of Congresbury station).

Sandford Station Railway Heritage Centre

The most complete Strawberry Line station buildings open to the public are found at Sandford Station Railway Heritage Centre in the former booking office of Sandford & Banwell station. The Grade II Listed building was sensitively restored as part of St Monica Trust's Retirement Village, and is a fine example of an early Bristol and Exeter Railway building. Volunteers have transformed the interior to create an authentic experience of a bygone era and bring the station back to life. The ticket office has been furnished with original equipment and outside the original 1869 running-in board has been restored to the station. The platform has a 1950s British Rail MK1 carriage and also a restored Sentinel shunting engine that worked into the station from the local quarry nearby.

The Centre is open at weekends and Bank Holidays from April to the end of October, and is accessed from the Strawberry Line. Entry is free. www.sandfordstation.co.uk

Winscombe Old Station Green

The former station site in Winscombe was in private ownership but thanks to the Millennium Green initiative, the community purchased it in 1999 to create a new public open space. The platform area, Strawberry Line track and other railway features have been restored, and visitors can see sculptures representing the former use of the site, the footprint of some of the old buildings and a timeline along the platform edge.

The site is managed by the Millennium Green Trust to contain areas for quiet relaxation, adventure, safe play and nature conservation. An annual May Fair is held on the Green to raise money for its upkeep.

Axbridge

One of the Axbridge station buildings can be seen on the Axbridge bypass and can be accessed from the back of the churchyard. It is now partly in use by a youth group. The bypass was built on the trackbed. The stationmaster's house is still in use as a private dwelling.

Cheddar
The station at Cheddar has lost its beautiful canopy but the building is now home to Wells Cathedral Stone Masons and surrounded by a small industrial estate. The buildings are used as offices and the old platform for works. The rest of the site was developed for housing and the stationmaster's house is now a private residence.

Draycott
At Draycott the station booking office and waiting rooms and the stationmaster's house were turned into private residences (opposite the Strawberry Special Inn). New houses were built on the track bed and at least one of them has incorporated railway memorabilia.

Lodge Hill, Westbury-sub-Mendip
The goods shed of Lodge Hill station, at Westbury-sub-Mendip, forms the core of a small industrial estate built on the old site. The old booking office and stationmaster's house have been dismantled but stone from the station was used in the construction of buildings at Cranmore, the main station on the preserved East Somerset Railway. The station canopy was re-erected on Westbury Playing Field where it still serves as a shelter/stage for village events.

The next railway bridge on Titlands Lane has been extended by a temporary structure and serves as the base for a carnival float.

Easton
There are no buildings at Easton but the deep cutting is still visible from the bridges at either end. Sadly it is in multiple ownership and although it is not used by most of the owners there is opposition to its use as a path.

Wookey Station – Haybridge

The railway buildings of the former Wookey station near Haybridge can be seen from the bridge over the former railway. They are now used by a local engineering company. From the other side of the bridge a short section of cycle path ends at Wells Leisure Centre.

Wells

Several of the buildings along the line from Wells can still be seen but are in use for other purposes. Starting from the Wells end there is a set of railway buildings at Haybridge, just after the current end of the cycle path, which can be seen from the bridge over the former railway. They are used by a local engineering company.

The next railway bridge on Titlands Lane has been extended by a temporary structure and serves as the base for a carnival float.

For information about the railway history of Wells, where there were three companies operating from different stations, see www.railwells.com

Wells to Shepton Mallet

From Wells going to Shepton Mallet most of the original trackbed is still in place and volunteers are working and campaigning to have it made into a cycle/walk route. There are no obstructions to building a path all the way to the centre of Shepton. The map on page 75 shows the progress of the route from Shepton Mallet west towards Wells.

Cranmore

The East Somerset Railway is a 4 kilometre (2.5 miles) heritage railway which was once part of the Cheddar Valley line. A section of the line has been preserved between Witham and Shepton Mallet. A working signal box dating from 1904 has been reconstructed in the standard GWR pattern. The preserved line runs through Doulting Railway Cutting – which is a Site of Special Scientific Interest.

Strawberry Line Path – Shepton Mallet

28 March 2015

The heritage railway has at Cranmore a recently restored classmate of the engine driven by Colin Forse through the snow drifts in 1963. No. 46447 was recently restored after being silent for over 40 years. The locomotive was built at Crewe in 1950 and withdrawn in 1966. It went to Barry Scrapyard but left there for preservation in 1972. www.eastsomersetrailway.com

Between Cranmore and the mainline, the railway still serves the quarry traffic from Merehead Quarry.

Further Reading

The Railway at Congresbury, pub 1986 Congresbury History Group

The Wrington Vale Light Railway, pub 1978 Michael Farr, Colin Maggs, Robert Lovell, Charles Whetmath

Great Western Railway Journal No. 15 Summer 1995

Branch Line to Cheddar, pub 1997 Vic Mitchell, Keith Smith

The East Somerset and Cheddar Valley Railways, pub 2009, Richard Harman

Steaming through the Cheddar Valley, pub 2001, Derek Phillips

A Life on the Railway, pub 2009, Colin Forse and Faith Moulin

The Wrington Vale Railway, pub 2004, Colin Maggs, Oakwood Press

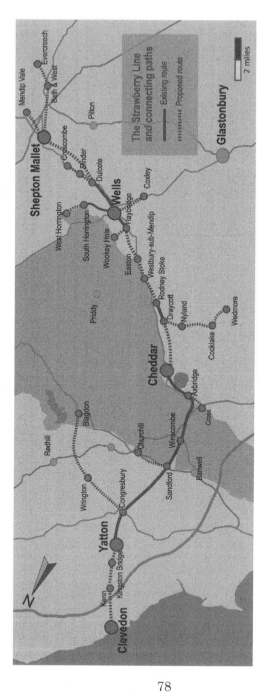

Map of Strawberry Line and its proposed development. Note – the villages marked with dots on the line did not all have stations on the original railway. Reproduced by kind permission of the Strawberry Line website: www.thestrawberryline.org.uk.